Psychic

The Ultimate Psychic Development Guide to Developing Abilities Such as Intuition, Clairvoyance, Telepathy, Healing, Aura Reading, Mediumship, and Connecting to Your Spirit Guides

Contents

INTRODUCTION 1

CHAPTER 1: WHAT IS PSYCHIC POWER AND HOW DO
YOU DISCOVER YOUR INTUITIVE TYPE? 2

    FOUR TYPES OF PSYCHIC INTUITION 7

        Clairaudience... 8

        Clairvoyance.. 8

        Clairsentience 9

        Claircognizance 9

CHAPTER 2: HOW TO DEVELOP YOUR PSYCHIC
ABILITIES 15

CHAPTER 3: PSYCHIC PROTECTION 29

CHAPTER 4: CLAIRVOYANT HEALING 41

CHAPTER 5: TELEPATHY 47

CHAPTER 6: GUIDED MEDITATION 52

CHAPTER 7: CONNECTING WITH SPIRIT GUIDES 57

CHAPTER 8: AURAS AND AURA READING 62

CHAPTER 9: MEDIUMSHIP 67

CHAPTER 10: DREAM INTERPRETATION 71

CONCLUSION 85

Introduction

The following chapters will discuss what psychic ability is, the four intuitive types, and the tools needed to help you develop your own potential for psychic premonition, healing, and protection from negative forces. It also provides instruction for contacting your Spirit Guides (also known as Guardian Angels), Guided Meditation, Mediumship, and Telepathy.

You will learn how to interpret the psychic and energetic messages you receive from others and from the spirit realm – as well as how to read people's auras, both visually and energetically. The goal is to start you off at the beginning of what is hopefully a long and fruitful journey to discovering and strengthening your psychic abilities by providing useful and detailed ways in which you can practice "flexing your psychic muscle". This book further explores different types of psychic readings – complete with examples and guides on how to interpret different signs.

Chapter 1: What Is Psychic Power and How Do You Discover Your Intuitive Type?

Real-life psychic abilities aren't really like what we grew up watching on TV. Psychics don't get a vivid flash into the future out of nowhere, like a little movie playing in their mind's eye, just in time to warn the subject of the vision so that they can change their fate – the ability to sense what the future holds isn't just the stuff of Hollywood. Although it's a lot subtler than how it's portrayed on TV, it's more of a heightened intuition.

Now, everyone has intuition, but some people's psychic intuition is stronger than others for a number of different reasons – the most common being that they don't exercise it much, as they usually don't believe in intuition, and as a result, don't listen to it or can't detect it. It could also be because of emotional blockage or trauma that leaves you unable to tap into your psychic channel and focus your energy properly. Therefore, it never gets developed and lies unused and dormant in a person's subconscious.

See, your intuition is like a muscle – you have to keep using it and practicing with it for it to develop into true psychic ability. If you've grown up in an environment where you were encouraged to trust your "sixth sense" as it were, you are more likely to have stronger psychic ability. But there's good news for those who were brought up by the skeptics of the world and/or if you're a skeptic yourself! Even if you didn't have this early exposure and permission to develop your gift, that doesn't disqualify you from achieving psychic power. For those of you in need of a bit of a spiritual workout, let's get started!

One thing people who are perhaps more in touch with their intuition often find themselves asking when they have a sense something is amiss is: am I just being anxious and paranoid, or is my sense of foreboding legitimate? The trick that usually works for getting to the bottom of doubt about your sense and whether it's just anxiety or an actual premonition is: if you feel a sudden flash of foreboding or some sense that something's going to go wrong and then it disappears – that's your intuition. Heed the feeling and listen to what it's telling you, what it's warning you of. It could be gravely important. However, it won't stay long, so try your best to interpret it while it's there – you can even write down how it feels. If you get a sense that something is wrong and just can't stop thinking about it all day to the point where you're overthinking it and overanalyzing it to try and figure out what it means and how you can solve it to the point that you're quite worked up and that it just won't go away – it's more likely just anxiety and not a true psychic prediction in this case. It's easy to tell when it's anxiety because the feeling just won't leave you alone.

Another sign that it's a psychic premonition would be a type of tingling feeling. Psychic premonitions are also generally accompanied by a feeling of tingling in your brain, usually on top or between your eyes. They don't *always* come with this feeling, but the chances are if whatever you think you're sensing is accompanied by tingling in your head, then it's fairly safe to say it's a premonition.

You may also feel very drained or low in energy after a psychic premonition, although this could be due to anxiety as well since stressing and agonizing over something can take a mental toll and make you feel exhausted throughout the day and afterward. Hence, this isn't a sure way to tell if it's a premonition, but psychic premonitions do make one feel tired, especially in the case of beginners, as they don't know yet how to use the energy of the universe for help.

Using just your own reserve of energy is usually not the best way to go about psychic practice, as it is limited (as opposed to that of the universe which is unlimited) and can/will be depleted very quickly. If you get a premonition out of nowhere (i.e., receiving a premonition even though you weren't attempting to receive one), it won't leave you a choice to be aided by the universe's energy – but if you are setting out to do a psychic reading, it is important not to use your own limited energy supply and attempt the reading and to receive premonitions unaided.

As you begin awakening your psychic powers, you will begin to notice some changes in your life. This is a sure sign that you're on the right track and that your abilities are growing. Keep an eye out for anything you notice about yourself that's out of the ordinary or if people say you seem different. This is likely because you are vibrating at higher energy now that you've begun to awaken your intuition!

Vivid dreams are one certain sign of this. You will probably notice that the more in tune you are with yourself and your abilities, the more vivid your dreams will be. If you are someone who rarely dreams at all, or rarely remembers your dreams (and if you do it's just vague images and feelings), you will notice an increase in your dreams, and you can recall them more vividly. This is because once your psychic powers have been awakened, your subconscious is more freed up and less blocked, so dreams flow more naturally. You can also receive psychic messages in dreams (see Chapter 10). Being more in tune with your intuition also heightens your energy, consciousness, and connection to the spirit world, which can present itself to you in your dreams now that your mind has been more awakened.

Along with vivid dreams and tingling sensations, you may also experience a higher frequency in headaches. If you do, please consult a doctor just to be safe. It could be a sign of your mental capacities straining themselves and becoming tired from the psychic practicing you have been doing. The amount of energy you have to use to connect with and focus on your intuition and the psychic realm is great, and even if you tap into the energy of the universe, it can still be a great strain and a burden for a beginner psychic's brain to bear. However, fear not – the headaches should begin to dissipate as you progress and develop your abilities and become stronger and more focused. Eventually, as you become more experienced and in touch with your intuition, psychic readings can become like second nature – and while they are likely still to be tiring, the headaches should subside unless you are doing a particularly difficult reading or a reading requiring a substantial amount of energy, focus, and time. If they do not cease, again, please talk to your doctor about your symptoms. This is important to remember for all symptoms, aches, and pains that can be associated with psychic reading, etc. It's always better to be safe and get them checked, as psychic ability is only one possible explanation.

You may also notice that your other senses become heightened now that you are on the path to psychic awareness. If you've noticed that you no longer need the subtitles turned on when you're watching a movie, your pallet has changed slightly, your eyes seem sharper than usual, or colors become more vivid, you're more sensitive to certain fabrics, and you can pick up and pinpoint scents with much more ease, this can be attributed to your increased psychic potential. After all, you're heightening your sixth sense; it's only natural that the others increase in ability as well. Now, if you get frustrated because you still need your glasses even though your psychic abilities are increasing, just remember that becoming a psychic isn't a cure to anything. It's not going to suddenly allow you to see with 20/20 vision or give you a refined pallet; it may simply elevate your senses slightly, that's all. It's just a sign of increased power.

The more your psychic powers start to show themselves, the higher your vibration becomes. The higher your vibration and energy become, the less time you will want to spend around negative people or doing negative things. Don't be surprised if, while on your psychic journey, your eyes are opened to the negativity and negative habits of some of the people in your life. This is a completely normal part of the psychic journey, and you may end up feeling the need to remove certain people from your life or cease doing certain negative activities that you used to partake in. Unnecessary drama, rudeness, gossip, harmful behavior, etc., are all examples of things which you will begin to have the strong urge to avoid or cease. This is not to say you can't indulge in your favorite reality TV show from time to time, or cut a friend out of your life because they are struggling with an addiction or because they are having a rough day and get angry at you or are negative in the sense that they are sad and maybe struggle with depression. However, people who are always constantly negative and want to drag others down with them are no one you want to be around. If it feels right for you and like it will ultimately bring you happiness and empower you on your journey, then it's best that you remove these people (as gently as possible, without being rude or mean about it, be polite and sensitive if you believe they are owed that) or stop doing these things which bring negativity into your life. Negativity is extremely draining to non-psychics so you can imagine what it does to someone who is likely going to be quite vulnerable to the emotions, thoughts, and energy of others. This is why it is best for psychics to avoid negativity.

An increase or development of psychometry is also common for new psychics. Psychometry is when you can sense the energy or history related to an object just by touching it. Eventually, you may even have premonitions associated with the object, but while you're still a beginner, you may just notice that you can sense the energy of a certain object, often not on purpose. This is quite common in antique stores. Brushing against an old silver mirror, locket, item of jewelry, or any sort of old heirloom may bring you an odd sense of longing seemingly for no reason, but this may be due to the history of the item or the item's owner. Perhaps the item was given to them by the love of their life who then died or left them or who maybe they were forbidden to see. This would explain the feeling of longing associated with the object. It usually occurs with older objects or objects which have been through a lot, and whose current or previous owners have been through a lot. It can be articles of clothing, jewelry, art, furniture – even when entering a house many psychics can feel the energy related to it and its history/old owners. If you are moving out soon and go to look at an open house, to get a sense of whether the house is right for you, also take into account the energy of the place. Run your hands over the walls, counters, and furniture in every room. This should give you a good indication of whether there is an excess of negative energy or not, or whether you/whomever you're moving with and the house will be a good energetic fit. You'll often hear of people's hair standing on end and having a sense of evil or negative energy when entering a house, and then later finding out a murder or some other horrific event took place there at some point. This is because they are picking up the energy of the space through psychometry. People with more developed intuition and psychic abilities are more prone to picking up energy, so if you begin sensing things like this when you touch them, it's a good sign that you're on the right track.

Four Types of Psychic Intuition

Now that we're discussing what your psychic intuition feels like and some signs that your powers are developing, let's take a look at the different types of psychic intuition and define them:

- Clairaudience
- Clairvoyance

- Clairsentience
- Clair cognizance

You may not have heard these terms before, so here is a brief description of each.

Clairaudience is when it sounds like someone is speaking directly in your mind. Not in the same way as people with certain mental illnesses – this is more of a short answer to a question, or advice, and it shouldn't sound/feel harsh or discordant. The word "clair" means clear, and "audience" is from "audire" meaning to hear, so you are psychically "hearing" these messages, though usually, it is within the mind. It can sound similar to when you act out a conversation in your head, or similar to how you hear people talking in dreams. These sounds and messages can come from your spirit guides or from the spirit of someone in your life who has died. If you've ever seen someone go to a psychic medium (Chapter 9) on TV, or perhaps you accompanied someone once, to try and contact a dead loved one, and the medium will ask them the meaning of a certain phrase or sound, they are likely receiving these through clairaudience.

Clairvoyance is when you see images in your mind's eye that hold psychic significance. "Voyance" meaning vision, so clear vision. The next time an image springs into your mind, seemingly out of the blue, try to analyze it. It may have a symbolic (or very literal) meaning about something coming up in your life, or it may explain something you've been thinking or worrying about. Clairvoyance won't be a very specific flash into the future where you can see exactly an event that will happen as a movie in your mind – like how they show it on TV shows. It will be a subtle image or "vision" in your mind's eye. You may have had clairvoyant messages in the past without realizing it! Some examples of what is classified as a clairvoyant message could be colors, numbers or letters, words, pictures or images of people, objects, animals, places, or anything symbolic.

Clairsentience (clear feeling) is probably the most common of the four. It is when you *feel* something is going to happen. If you've ever heard someone use the phrase "I can just feel it" or "this doesn't feel right" this is clairsentience. Clairsentience is often called your "gut feeling" or your instinct. Another aspect of clairsentience is being able to sense the emotions of others. Maybe you feel a wave of sadness before your friend walks into a room, and then they tell you their mother has passed away. Maybe you're on the phone with your friend who has a broken right leg, and you feel a brief pain in your right leg, even before knowing they broke it. Maybe you see your pet and suddenly burst into tears overwhelmed by sadness for no apparent reason, and within a week, your pet dies. These are examples of clairsentience.

Claircognizance (clear knowing) is when your intuition helps you figure something out that your rational brain can't, something you're maybe stuck on. For example, if you're stuck in traffic, should you risk taking the upcoming exit to get out of it and take the backroad, or will that end up taking longer? You inexplicably decide to wait it out and soon traffic has cleared, and you're on your way. This is claircognizance. If you've ever heard someone say, "I just know" and they have no evidence to prove their certainty or no way of knowing but end up being right – that is claircognizance.

So how do you tell whether you're just having an ordinary thought or whether it's a psychic message? The messages and premonitions can often be quite subtle, but the way to tell is if something (image, sound, feeling, certainty) just pops into your mind with absolutely no relation to what you were just thinking about. This is probably a psychic message and not a thought. Usually, these psychic messages are quite strong as well, not a little afterthought at the back of your mind. However, sometimes they are quieter communications, so with anything that comes into your mind seemingly unprovoked, it's always best to try and look at it closer and analyze it – it may have some psychic significance.

With these four channels of psychic communication, if you just take a deeper look at the next sound, image, feeling or thought that springs into your mind unbidden, you may find some relevant psychic meaning to it. The message(s) will help you gain information, receive communications from the spirit realm (spirit guides, passed on loved ones, etc.), or reveal premonitions or predictions to you, that your other five senses can't. You may already have read this list and honed in on one of the four that you feel more connected with or that you think one of them will definitely come more naturally than the others. Maybe you have used one or more of these in the past, whether you realized it at the time or not. Maybe you've already noticed that you have more of an ability for one than the others. That is likely the one you will be strongest at and the channel you will receive the clearest most powerful messages in, at least for now. I don't mean you can't practice with the other types and strengthening them. There are many psychics who, for example, started off naturally talented at clairvoyance and receiving clairvoyant messages, but as they practiced, they gradually became more powerful at, and mastered, clairsentience and that became their strongest intuitive channel. This is just one example, but it's to show that you're never stuck in just one situation or skillset with just one option! Although if you wish to keep the one you have a knack for as your strongest ability, then by all means. Remember, psychic ability is like a muscle!

Each psychic has a specific way in which their power and intuition manifests itself, and it's often related to who they are and what sort of person they are. Everyone, regardless of ability, has one of four psychic personalities. You are either a spiritual intuitive, a physical intuitive, an emotional intuitive, or a mental intuitive. So how do you find out which kind you are and fits your psychic abilities? Well, each one manifests itself differently, and there are certain traits associated with each type that you can look over to aid you in discovering which one you resonate with the most, and which one seems to be more *you*. There is no official test, but each psychic personality is defined in the following paragraphs – and hopefully, you can get a sense of which one fits for you.

Physical intuitives are the ones that have deep attachments to important objects, and usually, psychometry (sensing things via touching physical objects) comes naturally to them. They are the ones who are more likely to use objects like tarot cards, crystal balls, palm reading or tasseography (tea leaf reading) to determine things about a person or the future and perform psychic readings. They are very literally hands-on when it comes to sensing energy, relying on physical presence or moving their hands close to an object or person to get a sense of things. This makes them the ones most likely to be drawn to the art of psychic healing, or the ones that usually have a natural talent for the practice. They are often homebodies and love organizing their home, furniture, and decorations according to their interests. Their home isn't simply some space for them to eat and go to sleep at night – it is their temple and haven from the outside world, and it showcases a piece of who they are. They spend a solid amount of time at home and often have a lot of clutter and trinkets around the house. They also thoroughly enjoy spending time in nature and grounding themselves.

Mental intuitives are the analysts. They will think things over repeatedly, turning it over and over in their minds until they find an explanation for something until they yield a result. They always make sure they take into account every little detail, checking and double checking. They don't ever want to miss anything, and they're not big risk takers, nor are they very spontaneous. Mental Intuitives are more likely to be clairvoyant or clairaudient and receive psychic messages via imagery or sound in their mind, as this is where they spend most of their time. They tend to "live in their head" so to speak and can go for hours on end with merely the company of their own thoughts, just thinking. They are going to need the most information and ask for the most detail when they sit down to do a reading for someone. They are the ones to logic their way through something – logic, reason, and rationality are what they live by.

When working on something, whether it be a psychic related task or otherwise, they generally have a good ability to focus and stay focused on what they are doing. They also tend to have somewhat academic interests, although this isn't always the case.

Meditation is really important for *spiritual intuitives*. Aligning their energy harmoniously within themselves and with the universe is key to them. They are very aware of spiritual unbalance and they can sense it quite acutely. It can make them irritable and feel "off" and discordant until they meditate or find some strategy for inner balance, peace and grounding to set them in place again. They are less grounded in this world than the other types and would be described as the type to "have their head in the clouds," having a tendency for vivid daydreaming quite frequently. Their minds wander constantly, and they can have a tough time keeping focused on a task, including psychic readings and/or connections. They are the most connected to the spirit plane in most cases, being the people that, even with dormant psychic power, receive or are visited by spirits from the spirit realm, most commonly people they knew who died and passed over. Mediumship (Chapter 9) is often something spiritual intuitives are drawn to. Aura reading, energy healing, mediumship, and receiving psychic messages through dreams are all practices that, in most cases, come naturally for the spiritual intuitive. They tend to have quite vivid dreams with subconscious messages (Chapter 10). They can also have an affinity for traveling. They do need to be careful, though, as they are prone to addiction and escapism. They are also the most likely to worship some form of deity or higher power.

Emotional intuitives are the ones that can read or sense people's emotions with the most ease. Sometimes this can feel like a burden to them as they feel bombarded by other people's feelings and just want to tune it out, especially for beginner psychics/intuitives who are still figuring out how to turn these kinds of energetic messages "off" and "on". They may prefer small groups to large ones and really enjoy their alone time for this reason. They're your classic introvert, partially because being home alone for them works as a sort of haven away from all the different energies floating around in the world, a place where they can truly relax and tune out, not absorbing the different feelings of strangers in public. As the name suggests, they themselves are also very emotional and sensitive people. They are described by many as empaths, due to their extremely high empathy and ability to feel what others are feeling. Beyond just sympathy, they share whatever feelings someone may be having. These people have a natural predisposition to clairsentience (clear feeling). Their high empathy and understanding the different perspectives of others causes them to be people pleasers at heart. They want everyone to be happy, and they always strive to help people. They are the classic "shoulder to cry on" personality. However, it is very important that they don't allow this need to help and please others to take them over. They need to watch out that people don't attempt to take advantage of them, as is often the case when other more negative people sense that someone is empathetic/emotionally intuitive. Negative, cruel and manipulative people will energetically drain them dry if the emotional intuitive is not careful. They must avoid this type of person at all costs! It's important for them to learn that they need to stand up for themselves, say no, and take time for themselves. They make decisions based off of how they feel instead of using logic. They think with their heart, not their head. These people are natural storytellers, so you will often find them in professions such as writers, musicians, poets, and artists. Due to their selfless nature, you will also find them inclined to do psychic healing work, similar to spiritual intuitives.

Hopefully, these brief descriptions gave you some insight into what your intuitive type may be —although keep in mind that these are just basic outlines, stereotypes of which categories people may fit into. If you don't fit every description listed for each type that's fine; most likely no one is going to fit all of these traits. They're just to give you a sense of which one may connect and resonate more with you and describe you best. You may feel that one represents you more than the others. Your intuitive type is important to know because it tells you about how it affects your use of your psychic abilities and which aspects, techniques, and abilities may come more naturally to you.

Chapter 2: How to Develop Your Psychic Abilities

Now that we've gone over the four types of psychic messaging and you've likely found that you are stronger with one than the others, as well as having discovered your intuitive type, let's discuss how to practice and strengthen these abilities.

Get started on the road to feeling empowered and confident in yourself! Remember, even the most experienced or naturally gifted psychics didn't start their journey with complete confidence and power; they had to practice often to gradually increase their abilities. The key is to believe in yourself and stay relaxed. Trust in your ability and intuition, even though, if you've been raised to ignore it, it may feel silly at first. Keep noticing subtle things you sense. Additionally, keep in mind that you should keep practice sessions relatively short, no more than an hour, as longer sessions are unnecessarily draining and exhausting, and you can't be expected to keep your focus that long. Once you've lost your focus, concentration, and grounding, any practice you attempt will be ineffective.

A feeling of fear may arise as you begin to have more accurate premonitions. This is natural –you're now aware of a plane of reality that humans are not normally in tune with. Part of developing your abilities and confidence is overcoming this fear or uneasiness. If you truly want to become more powerful, fear will only get in your way. Reluctance will hinder you. It's true that not every prediction will be a positive one. You may foresee relationships ending or loss of money or death, and you must accept that these are all a part of life. You must be ready for negative premonitions as well.

Another important thing to remember is: don't let skeptics dissuade you. You'll know if you've had a psychic experience that even though it can't be explained by logic, there's no denying its truth. If there are many hardcore logical skeptics in your life, they may mock you or question you, trying to convince you that you're foolish or even crazy. It's important to remain calm and focused; don't let these kinds of people distract you or hinder your abilities. You'll find people like them everywhere, so try to block them out as best you can.

One great technique is writing down potential psychic messages. Try keeping a journal of what you think may be clairvoyant, audient, sentient or cognizant premonitions. Keep track of these recordings and see if anything ever becomes of them – if they're relevant at all. This is an excellent technique for beginners because you can sort out the random bits and pieces from actual psychic messages, and you can start to piece together what a prediction or premonition actually feels like. It may help you to write down how you felt beside each potential message as well.

This can't be reiterated enough. Practice every day. This may sound daunting, but if you keep it up, pretty soon it will come naturally, and you won't even notice you're doing it. Now, if you miss a day or two or more for whatever reason (illness, feeling emotionally drained, etc.), don't worry! Just pick up where you left off and keep testing different techniques and tools. It's not something to panic about if you haven't practiced in a while, you won't lose "the gift" as we all have it, just as your muscles won't deteriorate if you don't go to the gym for a while. This is just to tell you the best and most effective ways of developing your gift's power.

Another highly effective tool is Meditation. We'll go over it more thoroughly in Chapter 6, but we'll touch on it now as it is one of the main tools and techniques for developing your psychic intuition.

If you're practicing daily, try incorporating ten to twenty-minute meditation sessions into your daily routine before you try to interpret anything. This will clear out any emotional blockages, thoughts, worries, or distractions you may have both relevant to psychic practice or about your daily life. It also connects you to a higher plane where your spirit guide(s) and psychic energy reside. Connecting with your spirit guide(s) during meditation will also help answer any questions you may have, as they will help you. Meditation empties the mind to help you focus on the spiritual task at hand. For more information on meditation, meditation techniques and spirit guides, see Chapter 6.

Psychometry is also a really easy technique to try. The word may sound complicated, but all it means is reading the energy of an object. Just pick something up that has some meaning you know, like a family heirloom to start, and focus on the energy coming off of it. Clear your mind and see what comes up. Don't force any images, just let them flow. Once you've practiced like this a few times, try transitioning to an object you don't know the history and meaning of. Go to a thrift store and buy an old silver knick-knack or item of jewelry. Or you can ask a friend to lend you an important item of theirs or their family's without telling you the history and meaning behind it. This way, it's likely to be more effective as you can do the reading in front of your friend, telling them what images, words or feelings come up, and they can tell you whether they have any relevance or accuracy.

Notice certain symbols that reoccur in your premonitions. If you've done any preliminary research on prophecies or predictions, you'll probably have stumbled across some sort of symbol guide –for example, things like red means love, 13 means bad luck, green means wealth, etc. However, what you should know is that there are no universals! Symbols are different for everyone. Tied to the journal idea is the idea to try and keep tabs on what certain images, colors, or numbers tend to symbolize for you.

If possible, surround yourself with like-minded people, such as other psychics or people on the same spiritual path as you. If you find people on the same vibrational level, your energy will rise, and this will help you thrive spiritually. Thus, growing your psychic ability. It's also nice to have positive reinforcement from your peers. If you don't know anyone in your life with a similar idea of spirituality, try finding some online. Different groups or forums on social media can be just as helpful as face-to-face advice and conversation. You can even look up if there are any local groups where you live that you can join and take part in. Try looking for a group with a mix of experienced and beginner psychics. That way, you can get advice and ask questions of the more experienced members while not feeling too intimidated as you have other beginners to practice and compare notes with. Whether online or in your life, it's important to have positive support from like-minded people

Spending time in nature is also a stress reliever to help open your mind. Some of this may just sound like basic life advice that doesn't have much to do with psychic powers, but it's impossible to grow as a psychic if you are stressed and emotionally/energetically blocked. Nature is our roots. Nature was here before us, and it will remain here long after we pass. Walk around and realize that, despite all your worries, the trees will still stand steady. The wind will still blow. The world will not stop. Take in the peace and the ancient energy of nature and let that energy soothe and empty your mind. As discussed, an empty mind is the best way to start a psychic reading.

Ask questions of the universe frequently. Whether you're walking down the sidewalk and are wondering whether you should change careers, or you're relaxing in the bath, wondering if your relationship is working out? No matter where you are and what you're wondering, try to become aware of this and consciously ask the universe for advice. Take it out of the wondering state and purposefully ask the universe, what do I do? How do I figure this out? Get specific. You may not get an immediate answer, but if you wait, a day, a week, maybe a few weeks, the answer will likely deliver itself to you. You need only ask.

If you've been trying these techniques and feel like you're stuck with what to do next, just repeat, repeat, repeat, practice, practice, and practice. The path to developing your psychic powers is different for everyone, but the universal is to remain confident and focused. If there's one technique that feels like it works for you more than the others, focus on that one – whatever is working best to grow your powers.

Next, we will discuss some important tools psychics sometimes choose to use: *tarot, crystal ball scrying, palmistry*, and *tea leaf reading*. These are all forms of divination, a way of telling the future. There are other physical tools and methods that psychics can use but let's start with these four. You will likely prefer one over the others or find a certain method comes much more naturally and is easier for you, providing you with more accurate readings. Don't feel pressure to master all of these; they are just possible methods you can use as a psychic.

If you've ever heard of *tarot* cards, you may have heard that you can't buy your own deck; one has to be gifted to you. This is a myth. You can pick out and buy your own deck, and it won't change anything. When choosing a deck, try and connect with it – its energy has to click with yours. If the artwork really stands out to you, this is also a good sign that it's your deck. Once you have selected your deck, don't try and do any readings right away. You have to spiritually "break it in", so to speak. One way of doing this is taking each card out one by one, and passing it over smoke. This will cleanse its energy. Then, shuffle through the deck and examine each individual card, taking in any feelings the artwork may evoke. Go for a walk with your deck, sleep with it next to your pillow. It's important to intertwine your energies so that the deck is familiar with you and you with it. When you're just starting, you can do readings for yourself, and then maybe ask a friend if you can practice with them. When doing a reading, you can find a spread you like (for example three cards: one for past, one for present and one for future) and while shuffling/before spreading them out, ask the card a question. It can't be a yes or no question because there aren't yes or no cards. However, it can be as vague or specific as you like. If you are doing a reading for someone else, they may want to keep their question private, but let them know that this may make interpreting the message of the cards slightly more difficult. If you are reading for someone else, lay the deck in front of them and ask them to cut the deck into three piles, then choose the top card from each pile (this is one example of a basic spread. If there is another way you feel you want them to draw the cards, or if you want to draw for them, then go for it, there are many different techniques). When each card is flipped over revealing the artwork, check to see if any of them are upside down (decide first which way will be the right way up, facing you or facing them). Now, not everyone follows this belief, but many tarot readers read upside down cards differently than when they were the right way up. You can read them this way or ignore it. Your tarot pack should have come with a little book describing each card. If not, then you can go out and buy a tarot book from your local occult shop or bookstore or search online. The description is only half of it though. The next step is to apply it to the person's question/life and interpret it based on what they asked. If they do not wish to tell you their question, explain the meanings of the cards and where they sit in the spread as best as you can and check in with them to see if it's making sense and applicable to their question at all. Some readings will be extremely obvious in their message while others are more cryptic and take more analysis and introspection. To practice memorizing card meanings and descriptions, get into the habit of drawing one card every morning to see how your day is going to go. Pick your card and read the description for it. Pretty soon you'll get more familiar with the cards and their descriptions.

Crystal ball scrying is another classic tool used by psychics. It's such a famous item that it's made its way into many movies and it's a universal symbol of psychics. While it is such a famous symbol, it's an art that's tricky to perfect and most likely won't yield immediate or solid results. To start off, it's best to do crystal ball scrying in a dimly lit atmospheric space that will allow the mind to relax and wander. Large crystal balls can be quite pricey, but small ones work just as well and are much cheaper. Make sure it's a clear crystal ball and not made of an opaque stone, and that you have some sort of stand for it (wood, glass or stone is preferable to plastic) so that it doesn't just roll off the table. As you gaze into your crystal ball, your focus should be on the middle. Try to have some sort of solid background behind it so that you don't mistake the distortion of any objects or light for images. You should feel yourself entering an almost trancelike state, and it may take a few minutes for the ball to begin to reveal things to you. Remember, relaxation is the key. Light incense or diffuse essential oils and play calming instrumental music if you think this will aid you in getting to the proper state where the ball's secrets will reveal themselves. Take a moment to quiet your mind before you begin. Clear it of any hopes or expectations of what you think will happen or what you think you will see. Another thing to consider before you begin is, like with your tarot deck, spending time getting familiar with your crystal ball. Hold it, keep it near you, build up that connection. Now that you are ready, your mind calm, your atmosphere set, you can begin gazing. Make sure whatever position you're sitting in to gaze will be comfortable for an extended period of time as it may take a while for messages to be revealed, or if it's your first time, not at all, and you will have to remain in one position for a while to hold your focus. As you gaze, visualize that your mind is as clear as the crystal ball. You'll know a message is incoming when a mist begins to appear. When this happens, do not shift, either physically or mentally. Try to hold focus and keep the connection. Remain calm and still. You will feel yourself and your mind being drawn into the crystal ball, the ball and you are one. Images will appear, but don't interpret them yet. Just take them in, absorb them all one by one as they appear, until they start to fade away. This is when you can break your focus. Now you can reflect back upon all that you saw. Interpret the images as you would a clairvoyant message or a dream (see Chapter 10.) What did they symbolize? What were they trying to tell you (or the person you are doing a reading for) about someone, something, or some problem occurring in your life? How was this represented? If you are keeping a journal of your psychic practices and experiences, write down every image that revealed itself to you during your crystal ball gazing in as much detail as possible so that you don't forget, and so you can go back to them later and analyze it. Remember, the first time or even the first several times you may see nothing. Crystal ball scrying is a very tricky art to practice and hone, so just keep trying and do your best not to feel discouraged.

Palmistry (or chirology) is another famous symbol of psychic practice, and another useful tool many psychics use to perform readings. It is much easier to master than crystal ball scrying and cheaper than buying a crystal ball or tarot deck. All you need is a person who's willing to let you hold their hands for a short period of time, and that costs no money at all. You may have even seen your local psychic shop adorned with a neon sign of a hand with all the lines used by palm readers to tell you about your life. Each line represents something different about a person. There's the life line, the half circle starting from the middle of your hand and curving around your thumb. The head line and the heart line, which run parallel to each other (the head line is the lower one, the heart line higher, closer to your fingers). There is also the fate line which cuts through the heart and the head line, but not all people have a fate line. These are just a few of the most basic lines that you can interpret on someone's hand. The life line represents health, injury, major life events, and wellbeing. The head line represents how someone thinks and communicates, how creative or intellectual someone is, and how someone learns. The heart line represents emotion, romance, relationships, mental health, and heart health. The fate line shows how much of someone's life will be controlled by "destiny" or forces outside of their control. Look at your own hand and see if you can pinpoint each line. How you read them is based on how the line appears on the hand. Longer and curvier lines mean more emotional and creative, while straighter and shorter lines show a good handle on emotions and a logical disposition. Breaks in lines, especially the life and fate line, indicate major life changes. There are many books and websites online where you can read about how different lines appear to mean different things, but here are a few examples:

> • *Life Line*: the closer your life line is to your thumb, the more tired and low energy you tend to be. The deeper and longer a life line is, the more vivacity someone has. The shorter and shallower it is, the weaker willed the individual is. If your life line is straight and doesn't curve in towards the base of the thumb much, you are likely cautious when it comes to romance. A circle or island in your life line can indicate injury.

> • *Head Line*: If it's short, the person has more physical capacity than mental capacity. If it's separated from the life line, there's a love of adventure present. A curved head line indicates a creative individual. A wavy head line reveals a short attention span. If the line is deep and long, the individual is a clear and rational thinker. If it's a very straight line, they are a realist. If someone has a circle or cross in

their head line, this could be a sign of emotional trauma. A broken head line could be indicative of scattered thinking.

• *Heart Line*: If the heart line stops (or starts depending on which way you read it) below the index finger, the person is happy with their love life. If it stops below the middle finger, the individual is selfish when it comes to love and romance. If it stops in the middle of the hand, the individual likely has no trouble falling in love. If the line is very short and straight, the subject probably has no interest in romance. If the heart line touches the life line, has smaller lines crossing it, or is broken up, these can all be signs of heartbreak. If there is a circle or island in it, this can reveal depression or a period of sadness. If it is a long and curvy line, the individual is emotional, but if it's very straight and runs quite parallel to the head line, they can keep their emotions under control easily. If it's a wavy line, they most likely have commitment issues and have probably had many romantic partners.

• *Fate Line*: The deeper the line is, the more the person is controlled by "fate" and/or outside forces, while the fainter it is, the more control the individual has on their own life. If there are many breaks in the fate line, this shows life with many changes. If it is joined with the life line at the bottom, this shows someone who has a lot of ambition and is self-made. If it joins the life line in the middle, this shows an individual who has or will put their own interests aside for those of someone else. If it goes across the life line, this person will have a large support network throughout their life.

There is also a difference between which hand you read. Your dominant hand will be your past and present hand, revealing everything a person was born with. Your non-dominant hand will reveal everything that will happen in your future. So, whatever you see on their dominant hand is something that has already happened and tells you about them, while whatever is revealed on their non-dominant hand are things that could still be to come. To get the full picture and give the person the best reading you can provide, it's best to read both hands. These predictions aren't set in stone, however, and there can be signs in someone's hand that reveals the potential to change what the future will bring – for example, the fate line. Hand size also matters. Someone with smaller hands can usually be classified as a doer while someone with larger hands is more cerebral and takes less action. You can also find out how many children a person will have by balling up your fist. Turn it so you can see the folds your pinky makes. The number of free lines (not connecting the pinky to the palm) is the number of children you will have. This does not work with adopted children though.

Tea Leaf reading relies on symbolism and what the psychic interprets in the images the tea leaves create. This can also be done with coffee grounds, but tea leaves are the most traditional way used. You will have to pour yourself a cup of loose-leaf tea for this. It's obvious that a tea bag won't work. Drink the cup of tea you've made. It's okay if there's a tiny bit of liquid at the bottom, as this will help for the next step, which is to hold the cup in your hand a moment, ask it a question (no yes or no questions) and swirl the now empty cup (save the tea leaves) counterclockwise, three times. Now flip the cup upside down and leave it for a moment so that any excess liquid falls away. Turn it right side up again and take a look at what you see. Keep in mind anything that immediately pops out at you or any sense you get of meaning from your first glance. If nothing jumps out at you and it all looks very confusing and doesn't make sense, that's fine too – don't let it discourage you. You can look at the cup from different angles to see if anything changes or looks different. Take your time and examine all the shapes and clusters slowly and thoughtfully. Keep your mind clear and calm while doing a reading and focus on how the things you're seeing could relate to the question you've asked. Don't try to force a message. Common symbols you might see are crosses, stars, letters or numbers, anchors, or natural formations, such as trees or flowers.

There is no universal way of interpreting these symbols, but here is a list of some of the most common symbols and potential interpretations or meanings:

- *Ladder* – Success. Usually in your work life, but it could be any aspect of your life. You are "climbing" the ladder to success and achievement.
- *Gun* – This demonstrates a desire to take action. Something in your life is making you frustrated and angry, and you want to do something about it.
- *Snake* – This predicts hard times to come. Possibly to do with your career, possibly a life change on the horizon. Brace yourself for difficulties.
- *Mountains* – Mountains usually mean a journey you have to undertake or obstacles that you must overcome on your way to your goal.
- *Angel* – This is a symbol of being in touch with your spiritual side. You may be entering a time of spiritual transformation and peace of mind
- *Baby* – This is a positive symbol. The interpretation of rebirth is an obvious one, as well as a life change and good news. It could also be telling you a new opportunity could soon be yours.
- *Acorn* – The acorn is another common symbol seen in tea leaf reading. It is a sign that your hard work will be rewarded and that good news and opportunity are on their way to you.
- *Plane* – This symbol is telling you to break out of stagnation in your life if you wish for success. There may also be an unexpected journey or a time-sensitive decision ahead of you.
- *Anchor* – An anchor is a good sign. This shows that the relationships in your life, whether they're friendships, romantic commitments or family bonds, are strong and the

people in your life are loyal. There's a lot of love. It may also be a sign that a dream of yours will come to fruition.

- *Bird(s)* – Another positive sign, seeing birds in the tea leaves usually symbolizes that good news is on its way. It's a premonition of positive things to come. It also encourages decision making.
- *Fish* – Seeing fish can mean good luck or something to do with overseas, whether something/someone is coming to you or you are voyaging overseas.
- *Flowers* – Another omen of good luck. Flowers can also symbolize close platonic friendships if there are many of them or love.
- *Heart* – Happiness is coming into your life. This will be due to someone you have affections for (they don't need to be romantic necessarily) or due to coming into money. Or maybe both! You can dream, right?
- *Cat* – The image of a cat can mean treachery, betrayal, gossip, or unkindness or unpleasantness may be present in your life. It can also signify disagreements with family, or problems involving money.
- *Dog* – You may fail in something you have been attempting. A dog's image can also foretell an unhappy end to a romance, or again, problems with money.
- *Triangle* – An unexpected but good or lucky encounter.

Tree(s) – A tree or trees is a sign of happiness. Money is coming your way; you will be prosperous. You are likely to find yourself healthy and able as well as happy.

Remember not to force any images you want to see on the tea leaves. Let them appear to you naturally – don't try to see anything that isn't there or twist the images to fit your fancy.

The placement of the tea leaves and where they end up in the cup is also important. Tea leaves around the rim or handle are related to you (or the person who's receiving the tea leaf reading). They are also most likely to be representative of the present or near future. Whatever's in the bowl of the teacup represents things that will happen in the more distant future. Another interpretation is that the closer to the handle, the more positive the message. Whereas the further down in the bowl, the worse news it is. And usually, if it's in the bowl, it can mean that this will occur not to the subject of the reading but to someone in their life, a relative, friend, lover, or even acquaintance.

If you're getting discouraged and you feel like you're just not making progress or improvement, don't forget to look back and see how far you've come! It's sure to make you feel better to see the progress you've made, and how much more in tune you are with your intuition. Maybe you've honed in on your intuitive type or had a premonition that turned out to be true. Don't compare yourself to others! Whether they are more experienced than you or are beginners like you but seem to be making more progress, remember: everyone's path is different and unique! Focus on *your* path and *your* progress.

Chapter 3: Psychic Protection

Now that you're dabbling in the realm of psychic messaging and the spirit plane, it is important to recognize the potential risks involved and how to protect yourself from them. You are opening yourself up energetically and spiritually and are vulnerable to negative energies. Just as you would avoid and protect yourself from negative and nasty people, places, object, etc., in the physical realm, you want to protect yourself from these energies in the spiritual realm as well, and the first step to protecting and healing yourself from psychic attack is identifying what a psychic attack looks like.

Psychic attack is when someone sends negative energy or "spirits" to latch on to you, meant in a malicious and harmful way. They may not have even meant to or realized they were doing it. They may not even be intuitive or psychic at all. Psychic attacks can be willed onto you from someone who doesn't even believe in them; they may simply be hurling powerful negative thoughts and curses your way. A psychic attack doesn't just come from people though. When you meditate, and invite spirits into your space or ask them for advice, you must be specific in who or what kind of spirit you are asking, as if you leave your space open and leave your question general, some very dark "spirits" or energies could take advantage of this and enter your home, wreaking energetic havoc in your life and on your psychic abilities. This dark energy may throw off your psychic abilities, cause you to suffer emotionally, and cause chaos in your life. When you're a victim of a psychic attack, things just won't feel right. For whatever reason, this person or spirit wants or wanted to hurt you, and you need to know how to defend yourself in case of a psychic attack.

How do you tell whether you're the victim of a psychic attack or just going through a rough spot in life? Some symptoms of psychic attack can include: nightmares, particularly very vivid nightmares, fear of a specific room in your home, sensing a presence/a feeling of being watched, bad luck, sudden illness, depression, and/or exhaustion, things falling over in your home even though no one touched them, feeling like your energy has been drained, inability to focus your power, feeling goosebumps or a draft of cold wind coming from somewhere unknown, feeling disempowered and low self-esteem. Please keep in mind that these are not guarantees that you have been targeted for a psychic attack; many of the things on the list can just be a part of life. Neither is this a comprehensive list. However, keep an eye on whether some/all of these symptoms are occurring in your life and whether these feelings are normal for you or are coming seemingly out of nowhere. If you have all or a lot of these, the chances are that it's a psychic attack. If you're normally someone with bad luck and nightmares, then perhaps there is no supernatural force behind it. If you are a paranoid person that always feels like you're being watched, then it's likely that there is no nefarious foe behind these feelings. However, if many of these occur together and it's highly out of the ordinary, it wouldn't hurt to start putting up some psychic protections.

The fastest and easiest way to repel negativity is through visualization, though it takes a lot of energy. There are a few different ways you can visualize this. One example is: if you sense negative presences or energy surrounding you, simply close your eyes and imagine you are surrounded by radiating blinding white light (or a color of your choice that symbolizes power and protection for you). Breath in to harness the energy of this light surrounding you, feel its power filling your body. And when you exhale, imagine that light is shooting out to envelope everything in your radius in a blinding flash, blasting all negativity far away from you, so that for a moment, your whole vision is white. Inhale as the light fades and you are standing calmly in your mind's eye. Repeat as many times as necessary to feel as if the negative presence has parted. You can also create your own visualization to repel negative forces. Just remember to channel a lot of energy into it; otherwise, it won't do much more than a daydream would. Don't use your own energy but rather tap into the universe's energy so that you don't drain yourself.

If you find that your psychic abilities are becoming quite strong and you are being bombarded by psychic "sixth sense" information at all times, a helpful tool to block out the overload of info is silk. Try wearing a silk scarf loosely around your head or draped over your shoulders and chest. Silk also helps defend the wearer from psychic attacks and block out any attempted psychic attacks.

Incense is also a good way of defending or healing from psychic attack. The smoke from incense cleanses your space and drives out negative energies. Try regularly lighting incense to keep your home cleansed. Or, if you think you are the victim of a psychic attack, light incense every day, especially in any rooms you feel a particular sense of negativity, evil, or negative energy buildup due to negative spirits/entities setting up camp in there. Keep doing so until you feel the ebb of these negative energies, and you and your home are spiritually restored and cleansed. You can also meditate or sit in front of incense to cleanse your spirit and clear your mind, but make sure there's proper ventilation. Otherwise, the smoke will go straight to your lungs, and the negative entities won't be driven out because there is nowhere for them to go – they will linger in your space. If it's cold, this doesn't mean open all the doors and windows – just have a fan going or crack a window slightly until the incense goes out.

Another protection you can wear/carry with you is gemstones. Certain gemstones, such as the powerful black tourmaline or obsidian, have properties that repel negativity and psychic attacks. Here is a list of some amazing gemstones for preventing and defending against psychic attack:

- *Tiger's eye*: Tiger's eye is a powerful and effective stone for blocking psychic attacks directed at you from other people. It repels the evil eye and leaves your attacker powerless to harm you.
- *Amethyst*: Amethyst is sort of an all-purpose gem, but it's great for dissipating negative energy, specifically negative energies directed at you in this case. It transforms them into something more positive.
- *Garnet*: The element of the garnet gemstone is fire. This stone will burn up and evaporate negative spirits and energies attempting to enter your home. It works as an excellent shield.
- *Lapis Lazuli*: Lapis Lazuli will strengthen your confidence and break down insecurities. It absorbs negative spirits and energies and then filters them out, making them weak and harmless. You won't even notice they were ever there.
- *Black Tourmaline*: As mentioned previously, Black tourmaline is considered by many to be the ultimate protection stone, especially against psychic attack. This is good news for you. It is a fast acting stone that will neutralize and break up any negative energies or entities headed your way. They won't even make it anywhere near you.
- *Hematite*: This stone, similarly to garnet, will act as a shield against negative presences and energies attempting to get at you. It is an extremely powerful shield, and it is also

associated with the earth element, making it good for grounding.

• *Labradorite*: A shield against psychic attack as well as a protection against any harm or bad wished upon you by another.

• *Black Obsidian*: This is a great stone if you believe you are being targeted by someone very powerful, someone with a lot of psychic power that you're unsure if you can match. This is a great stone for blasting away their attempts at a psychic attack, and a sort of bonus benefit is that it counteracts bad luck!

• *Peridot*: A great stone for protection against people who really drain your energy. This stone is less for protection against an attack and more for when you're going to spend time with someone whom you know has very negative energy and usually leaves you feeling quite low in energy and drained afterward – whether it's someone you care for, a friend going through depression perhaps, or a family member whom you find manipulative and never has a nice word to say or a boss that doesn't give you the respect you deserve as an employee. Whoever it is, this stone will protect you from their usual effects.

• *Quartz*, like amethyst, is another very general use stone. It dissolves negative energy and transforms it.

• *Smokey Quartz*: Smokey quartz, if you want to get more specific than clear quartz, is a very powerful stone. It has a high capacity for protection, as well as having healing properties. It also aids with anxiety, doubts, and self-esteem issues. It brings clarity of mind and empowers its wearer.

• *Turquoise*: This stone is a healing stone. If you are the victim of a psychic attack, try wearing turquoise on your person. It will protect you and dissipate any negative energies surrounding you.

Salt: Salt is a handy tool to use when protecting against negative energies as its energy absorbing properties are great. When calling on spirits in any way – whether you're doing mediumship (Chapter 9), asking your spirit guides for advice (Chapter 7), or inviting a spirit into your space or interacting with spirits in general – try keeping some salt around. You could keep a little sachet of it on your person, you could sprinkle it around yourself or your room (a less messy way of doing this is absorbing it in water and spraying it around you or your space), putting a small pile in the four corners of your house or room, or sprinkling some across windowsills and doorsills.

Keep these stones on you, around you, or in your home/space at all times and you may not even notice negative presences, energies, or spirits that try to harm you, and you will find yourself blissfully unaware of any attempted (and thwarted) psychic attack. Just remember: your stones are absorbing all these blows so they will need to be cleansed from time to time. This can be done by passing them over incense, leaving them out in the moonlight or sunlight (sunlight can fade colorful crystals like amethyst, however, so don't use this technique for such crystals), burying them in the earth for a period of time, or leaving them out in the rain (again, check to make sure the crystals you leave in the rain or water aren't water soluble). You can also energetically cleanse them and draw out all the built-up energies within them. See Chapters 4 and 8 for more on how to do so. These are just some of the ways you can cleanse your crystals – pick whichever method you wish to use or whichever one feels more right to you.

You can also hang mirrors from your windows or place shards of mirror in your lawn to mirror back any intended harm to where it came.

You can ask your spirit guides (see Chapter 7) for help defending yourself against attacks. Be sure not to demand anything from them

– ask nicely as you would ask a mentor for help. Remember, your spirit guides are looking out for you; they're on your side. If the attack is powerful, you may need the extra support. If you have someone in your life who also has psychic abilities, confide in them – maybe they can offer some helpful energy in combatting the attack. The mirrors' reflective surface should be facing outwards, away from you. This way all negative energies and spirits can be successfully reflected away and bounce off the mirrors.

Symbols and Sigils are also excellent for protection. You may have heard of people talking about their lucky horseshoe or their lucky underpants or what have you. You may have heard people say, "I won't go and do such a dangerous task without my lucky item/symbol." A symbol of protection can be anything. A pentagram is used for protection by many people who follow pagan beliefs. This is the five-pointed star facing upwards, surrounded by a circle. Many religions and cultures have important sigils of protection. Find a symbol or create your own, and draw it, carve it, sew it, or trace it with your finger or a crystal or incense stick onto something. For protection against psychic attack, a good strategy is to sew it into your pillow because that is where your head rests at night and your mind is, of course, going to be the target of psychic attack. Once you've found your psychic symbol, you must charge it energetically. This means you're going to want to focus on what you want this sigil to accomplish and direct this energy and goal onto the sigil. Focus your energy and your desire for this sigil while holding it in your hand, touching it, or tracing it over and over with your finger to physically transmit your energy and wish onto it. You can even speak out loud what you want from the symbol of protection, what its goal or purpose is, and what it should be doing. This is just another way to manifest your wish for it to protect you energetically. Get specific with your task for it as well. Make sure to include that you want it to protect you from psychic attack, ill will wished upon you, any negative energies, spirits, entities, and people that wish you harm, and to keep your mind, body, soul, and energy safe and ensure your wellbeing. You can, of course, make your own chant or mantra to speak to it, but these are just suggestions for some things to include.

If you have already become the victim of a psychic attack, the next step is to heal from it. Some techniques were mentioned in the paragraphs above, but let's really get into what needs to be done to heal from a psychic attack, as the effects can be quite devastating.

You are likely to feel quite violated after a psychic attack so try to ground yourself. Meditation, introspection, positive thoughts, and support from your loved ones will be essential at a time like this. Don't allow yourself to spiral out of control. Breathing exercises along with meditation will help greatly to keep your psychic channels clear. Do not succumb to the dark energy that has been sent to you. That is what your attacker would want. If you know who your attacker is (or have a suspicion at least), you can visualize them surrounded by light and positive energy. Sending this image out into the universe will help manifest the shutting down of this person's negative powers, and weaken their resolve to do harm and send out negativity. If you believe your attacker to be supernatural in nature, this technique also applies to harmful spirits and negative entities. If you're having nightmares, write them down and analyze them – it may make them seem less fantastical and frightening, and they may symbolize and reflect issues, worries, and problems in your waking life that need to be worked through. If you are feeling an energy drain or sudden depression, confide in someone and try and find the best ways that work for you to help boost your energy. Remember: this is a spiritual attack, so focus your healing on your spirit, energy, and emotional wellbeing.

You may feel anxiety and tension. It may be hard to recognize when you're right in it, but it can be comforting to have the knowledge that these anxieties and panics aren't rooted in anything rational. This is a symptom of the psychic attack and recognizing symptoms is half the battle. Just knowing that your anxiety, though it feels very real, is nothing to worry about may not stop the feeling – but hopefully, at the back of your mind, there will be some slight relief knowing that it isn't rooted in anything real, no matter how unpleasant it will feel while experiencing it.

Give yourself a break. If it's possible, take time off from any activities to heal and recuperate. There's no sense dealing with all of life's problems AND a psychic attack, which is when you're at your lowest, at the same time. This includes taking a break from your psychic practice! Consider it a spiritual sick day.

Try not to get sucked into the victim mentality. It's so easy to go down that road, but again, ground yourself. Remind yourself you are strong. Find a visualization that works for you where you are repelling the negative energy with your positive force, inhaling and exhaling. Becoming a victim wallowing in your symptoms is playing into what your attacker wants. You become weaker and more susceptible to their attacks. If your symptoms get serious, don't ignore them, of course. Take care of yourself. But don't let them drown you. Find the strength within yourself, tap into the universe's infinite energy, build yourself up and heal. Don't let fear rule you.

Overcoming fear is easier said than done, of course. Fear from psychic attack, "evil", or negative energies and presences, feeling overwhelmed by your premonitions, or fear of a prediction of bad news are big concerns for most up and coming psychics. Part of what you need to remember before you get started in overcoming fear is that your spirit guide/s and/or guardian angel is keeping an eye out for you; they are watching out for you.

Addressing fear of negative spirits and psychic attack is pretty straightforward: if you are on a positive path and do not set out to maliciously harm or wrong others, or dwell in negativity, negativity will not be drawn to you. Now, this doesn't mean that you should constantly walk on eggshells and let people walk all over you. If someone has wronged you or another greatly, you can and should stand up for yourself and defend yourself/them. Likewise, not dwelling in negativity doesn't mean not allowing yourself to have bad days or negative thoughts. It just means surrounding yourself with positive supportive and caring people, and not letting these low moments in life suck you down and change you for the worse.

The reasons why someone would want to send a psychic attack your way are numerous. Perhaps they are jealous of your success or relationship, or are angry at you for something, or are afraid of you, or are discovering and relishing in their dark side, etc. Whatever the reason, recognizing you have been targeted for psychic attack is one of the first steps towards healing from it. The confusion you feel surrounding the symptoms of your attack is half of what the attacker wants you to feel, and that's what makes these attacks most effective. Knowing that you've been attacked takes away this power from them, and now you can take charge. Now, you are in control.

Psychic attack isn't the only thing psychics have to worry about though. This isn't to try and dissuade you or put you off of following the psychic path, but simply to make you more aware of all the potential problems, fears, and dangers that may arise along the way as you walk this path. It's better to be aware of what may come up and how to deal with these things, then be blissfully in the dark until you have a negative encounter or experience, freak out, and become completely disillusioned with the psychic path.

The fear of being overwhelmed by your gift and being bombarded by constant psychic messages and premonitions is a common one. Beginners are particularly susceptible to this as they don't know how to rein in their gift yet. Try asking the universe for help with this. Focus your mind and state clearly (in your mind) that you do not want to receive premonitions and psychic knowledge constantly. Practice turning your gift energetically on and off, open and shut. When you want to begin reading, focus your mind, and ask for the universe's knowledge to flow again. Close your eyes, clear your mind, and ground your energy before and after using your abilities. The key is to stay relaxed and open when you are ready to receive psychic knowledge, premonitions, and messages again, and then to allow all the chatter and distraction in your brain to wash back in when you are ready to turn your gift "off". The more experience and power you gain, the more in control of your abilities you will be. It just takes time.

Something many people forget about is that psychic readings can bring bad news as well as good. This is worrying to some psychics who find it useless if there is no way to prevent this premonition from coming true, or who simply do not know how to, and hate to tell the person they are doing a reading for of this inevitable bad or harmful event that is likely going to occur to them or a loved one, or manifest itself in some way in their life. If you wish never to receive messages, predictions, or premonitions of bad things to come, especially if they are completely unpreventable, you can ask for this to be shut off. Whether while meditating and communicating with spirit guides or while focusing your energy and very clearly asking the universe, you can work on closing these channels. Consider before you do this, though, that maybe these messages are going through you for a reason. Say, for instance, you are quite adept at predicting deaths that are going to occur in the near future. You get a sense that someone is going to die soon. Maybe you have an idea of who or maybe you don't (which is even worse because then you really can't do anything or even warn the person or their loved ones). You see this power as pointless, but perhaps the reason you have it is that you act as a bridge between our world and the spiritual plane – our world and wherever the dead may go on their journey. You may be a great comfort to the dead, helping them on their path to crossing over into the next life. This is just hypothetical, but however your gift may manifest itself, it may have some meaning or purpose for doing so, or for showing you/telling you such things. Whether this is a responsibility you want or not is another thing, and remember you are not obliged in any way to take on any sort of spiritual role or pathway.

Now you know a bit about the dangers, fears, and obstacles of psychic work and a few tips and tricks to help you combat them and empower yourself. Hopefully, none of this has dissuaded you from continuing on your path to psychic power and ability. Your potential for great power is there, and as you practice, you will see your confidence increase and your ability to combat these fears, anxieties, and psychic attacks from others will grow. Eventually, people won't even think about sending negative forces or energies your way. Keep up with your practice and follow these techniques for protection, and remember that the odd fear or negative force creeping into your life is natural and just a part of the psychic path that you will have to overcome. You just have to have confidence in your abilities and believe in yourself.

Chapter 4: Clairvoyant Healing

If you've decided to awaken and strengthen your psychic abilities, you are probably in tune with your compassionate side. If you're like most psychics and want to use your gift to help people, you can use clairvoyant healing – also known as psychic healing – as well as giving them psychic readings. People who have a desire to become psychics or have a natural predisposition to psychic ability are naturally compassionate and empathetic people, so it's no wonder that a great many of them decide to become healers and help others. This may be something you wish to pursue, or perhaps not – but either way, this chapter will cover the basics of psychic healing so that you can begin helping others.

What you're doing when you're healing someone using your psychic power is sending them and their body healing energies. You're basically balancing and harmonizing their body's energies and removing blockages to dissipate physical aches and pains. It's a system of energy work where you are sending specific healing energy to the person who needs it. Clairvoyance comes into play because clairvoyant premonitions often help psychics by showing them images of the problem that can help them come to the solution of how to go about healing them. Psychic healers will also send someone clairvoyant healing images to manifest their "patient" as healthy, happy, and mentally, physically, and spiritually well.

To start healing someone, it can be helpful to meditate. You may even be visited by that person's spirit guide (see Chapter 7), giving you advice on what the problem is and how to handle it. Whether you've received a clairvoyant premonition, or you were told by them or their spirit guide what they need specific healing for, focus on your subject. It is best if the person you are healing is in the room with you, especially when you're first starting this healing journey. Clear your mind of anything except what you are trying to heal. With every inhale, you are drawing the unhealthiness out of that person's body, with every exhale, you are releasing it into the universe to be transformed into something positive. Draw on the Universal Energy as a source of power to help heal this person, as this can be a very energy depleting process if you work unaided. Visualize images of health. Imagine that they are the image of perfect health, from their head down to their toes. Start from the head, picturing them smiling and relaxed, breathing naturally, a glow radiating from them. Work your way slowly down the body picturing each body part in perfect working condition, even if that part is already healthy. The body must work as a whole – strong arms, heart beating steady, smooth skin, and sturdy legs that can carry them as far as they need to go in life. Keep picturing each part all the way to the feet. Imagine the area that's troubling them as a dark spot on their body. Dissolve it with your energy, watch it dissolve and fade away with pure light, leaving a radiant white glow behind. Then release and send this image of health via energy and clairvoyance to the person you are healing. They may not be able to see them consciously, but the energy and focus you put into them of healthiness will merge with their energy and their mind, showing their subconscious what they are working towards. It will manifest itself as you have also sent it out to the universe.

It is theorized that physical ailments can all be traced back to mental turmoil. Of course, if an outside factor has a hand in things, then this would not be the case. For example, a broken leg is not due to depression; it's due to your subject tripping or falling and the bone breaking. 24-hour nausea directly after eating at a two-star restaurant is probably not because of an inner battle with stress over a work decision – more likely it is food poisoning and nothing deeper is going on in these cases. However, with things like headaches, joint stiffness, muscle pain, intestinal problems, frequent nausea, etc., it is always worth examining a person's mental state. Is there a lot of built up repressed emotion? Depression? Worries and anxiety? Stress due to day-to-day problems or big decisions and events coming up in a person's life? These can all show themselves in physical ways as persistent ailments in the body that just won't go away. Usually, a certain point of physical pain is indicative of energy blockage. So, remember when you're healing, you're not just healing the body; you are also healing the mind. It's always worth it to consider the mental state.

There is no person alive who has suffered nothing and has no emotional issues that cause hindrances in their life. Every single person has been through hard times – although some more than others – but it doesn't invalidate the lasting effects it can have on the mind. When doing mental healing, keep in mind that everyone's been through different things and are dealing with different things in their current life, so don't treat every healing session the same, just as you wouldn't heal a headache the same as a sore stomach. Ask the person you are healing to look into their mind. What is or has been their mental state recently? If they don't want to tell you then that's fine, just have them acknowledge and be aware of anything that comes up and feel the energy of it. As this occurs, you may begin to pick up on a shift in energy. The psychic healer's job is to heal those physical ailments that have an emotional or mental origin. Focus your clairvoyant image messages on what the person is feeling now. Did you sense sadness or depression? Send to them visualizations of them happy and surrounded by a warm glow, perhaps running through a field of yellow flowers. Did you pick up on anxiety or worries? Imagine them completely at peace, eyes closed, face and body relaxed, breathing calm. Maybe they are in a mountain cabin with a cup of tea, nothing but nature around them. Tension and stress? Imagine them going through their hectic day-to-day routine with light ease, the chaos of their duties not phasing them. They are laughing and smiling and almost gliding or floating as they go through their day, light as air. These clairvoyant images will help their subconscious to release and let go of tensions that have been weighing them down and thus will help with whatever the physical symptoms they're experiencing are.

When you have finished a healing session, ask the person you were healing how they felt afterward. Did they feel relaxed? Did a peace of mind come over them? Any bodily sensations? Did any emotions come up for them? How about energy levels? Do they feel like they have more energy, less energy, or the same? Get feedback from this person and follow up a few days after the session to see if any improvements have come up or remain. If it was a specific physical ailment you were treating, ask how it felt immediately after the session and then follow up a few days later to see if your healing had an effect on it, if there was any improvement, and if it's lasted. Remember, you may not have a great effect right away. And if someone improves but it doesn't stick, remember it may take a few sessions – it usually can't just be done in one.

When you are psychically healing someone, be aware that it may take multiple sessions, especially if it's something more serious. However, as a beginner, it's best if you work with smaller less serious ailments to practice. You also have to note that the person you are healing has to want to be healed for your energy to have an effect. They may even say they want to be healed, but deep down, they don't want to be, or they are skeptical. If that is the case, then they will be a struggle to heal, and it may have no effect at all. Just make sure that you don't accuse your very first "patients" of not wanting to be healed because this may be due to your beginner status and inexperienced powers rather than their disbelief or subconscious unwillingness.

You can also clairvoyantly heal someone who isn't near you. In fact, they could be quite far away. This is described by many as praying. What you are doing is the same as if the person was in the room with you; you are sending them energy and clairvoyant images to heal. Try healing from a distance once you've practiced and built up your power healing someone in physical proximity to you. Since they won't be with you physically and you can't feel their energy present, you will have to visualize them more vividly and strongly. Picture every detail of them, and really put a lot of depth, detail and focus into the image of them as healthy and healed. Visualization is the key to distance healing since you don't have their energy to work with. You can even speak what you want for them out loud. The energy of your words will be released into the universe and solidified, manifesting these results of health for your friend or person whom you're trying to heal. Remember: when psychic healing, if you only rely on your own energy reserves, you will become drained quickly. Tap into the universe's energy; it will be an invaluable source of aid during your healing session.

If you want a test subject who won't demand results and won't complain or be skeptical, try with your pet. Maybe they aren't in need of healing but try sensing their energy, and through meditation, focus on your pet and specifically the health of your pet and see if any clairvoyant messages show up. If not, it's still a good way to practice getting a sense of someone else's energy and emotional state, as animals feel things just like we do.

Hopefully, this chapter has awakened you and opened your eyes to the source of many people's physical troubles. Whether you want to become a clairvoyant healer or not is of no importance. Not all psychics choose this path, though they may dabble in it. And choosing this path does not mean giving up every other aspect of psychic ability. It is just one ability that a psychic can develop. If this interests you, practice, practice, and practice – and don't forget to get permission from a friend, partner, or family member to practice your healing on them. Probably best to practice on someone who *has* some sort of physical ailment. Happy healing!

One last note for this chapter: it is extremely important that you are aware that psychic healing is not a cure. You CANNOT make diagnoses through clairvoyant psychic healing. Leave diagnosing patients to the professionals! It is highly unlikely that psychic healing will cure physical ailments completely or can be substituted medicine for illness and pain or medication and therapy for someone with a mental disorder. It can alleviate symptoms, get to the root of problems, get energy flowing and balanced again, and bring up someone's energetic frequency, but it should not be used instead of modern medicine or as a replacement for it. Rather, it should be used alongside it – they can work together.

Chapter 5: Telepathy

Have you ever watched a movie where two people communicate just with their minds or where someone reads another person's thoughts to gain information? Have you ever wished you could do that? Telepathy (from the Greek "tele" meaning "far away" and "patheia" meaning "to be affected by") is communication between minds – but like all aspects of psychic ability, it's not exactly how it's depicted in the movies. However, it is possible to practice telepathy in real life; it's just subtler. You may have even done so without meaning to – for example, if you've ever been thinking about someone or really wishing to hear from someone, and soon after they call or text out of nowhere with no previous planning. This is a form of telepathic communication. The two of your minds were communicating without knowing it, causing the person who called you to make the decision to call – or maybe their decision to call is what brought them into your mind and got you thinking about them. It's no coincidence when things like this happen. There are always psychic channels at work in situations such as these, and like psychic premonitions, everyone has the ability to use telepathy; it's just an area in our mind that needs to be exercised but that most of us ignore or don't believe in due to how we were raised, the society or religion we were brought up in, etc. Those that have been brought up encouraged to expand the mind and pursue psychic and telepathic abilities will have an easier time with this, but that doesn't mean those who were not can't succeed.

When using telepathy, it may not be possible to carry out a full conversation with your BFF using just your minds, but you can transmit images, words, or feelings to one another. To start, let your friend know that you want to try communicating with them telepathically. This is important especially when you're beginning because you will both need to be in a relaxed, focused and receptive state. You can try meditating or deep breathing before to prepare so that your body and mind are relaxed. They don't have to be in the same room or space as you; they can be at their house or even in another town. Close your eyes and try to tune out any background noise or distractions, and really focus your thoughts on your friend. Visualize them clearly in your mind's eye – their essence, their presence, details of their physical features. Once you have solidified this visualization of them as if they are almost there with you, visualize the word, image or feeling you want to send to them. Solidify it, make it vivid in your mind's eye. Make it your mind's only focus. Now visualize your friend, and visualize communicating this image to your friend. Imagine them receiving your message. They should have their mind open and receptive to your message at this point, and they should be visualizing you in their mind's eye. Once you've done this, relax, and let your message drift to the other person. Let it drift from your mind. At this time, you can relax your energy and focus. When the exercise is complete, follow up with them and ask them what they thought or saw in their mind's eye. Make sure to clarify that they shouldn't force any messages; they should just let their mind flow where it will and keep track of what may pop up.

Don't get discouraged if it doesn't work right away. It will take practice and possibly many tries. This is just one way to begin practicing, but no matter how you practice or whom you practice with, stay relaxed (both physically and mentally) and keep your mind open and receptive for both sending and receiving messages.

It's important to be in an environment that is totally comfortable, familiar and relaxing to you, to avoid the risk of distraction or being snapped out of your focus by strange noises, people, smells, etc. When you are just beginning your telepathy journey, and you've just started to practice, the best place to start is in your own home, maybe your bedroom or a room you find particularly relaxing. If your house is hectic and chaotic or you just can't feel relaxed there, try your backyard or a quiet park somewhere in a natural setting. Nature can help ground you and energize your powers. As long as it's a place you can tune out effectively, it should work.

The other commonly known aspect of telepathy is reading the minds of others. Telepathy is harder to practice on strangers, so again first practice with someone you are close with – a willing friend, family member, or partner. When attempting to read their mind, make sure to ask permission. Mind reading won't reveal to you a play by play of what they are thinking, but it will give you a vague idea, sense, or maybe a word or image related to what they are thinking about. Again, the same as with telepathic communication, you want to be in a setting that relaxes you. Close your eyes, tune everything out, and focus your energy on the person whose mind you are trying to read. Get the other person to picture something simple like a banana, and really focus on it. Obviously, they can't tell you what they are thinking. Once they confirm they have solidified their image, visualize them, try and connect with their energy, and let your mind flow. They do not necessarily have to connect with you or be on the same energy level for this practice because, as opposed to if they were sharing their image with you via telepathic communication, mind reading is more of a one-way street/one-man job. Make a note of all the things that flowed easily – not forced – through your mind and check in with them to see if you got anything right. Say, for instance, you saw the color yellow, or smelled banana bread, or felt disgusted (maybe they hate bananas). Don't be discouraged if you didn't get anything right the first few times you try this.

An additional way to practice with someone you know is to prepare yourself accordingly but then ask them a question out loud. Tell them not to answer it but just think about and process how they feel about it and what they would answer to it. It can't be a question you know or suspect the answer to. Right after you ask it, they will likely have an immediate reaction and/or thought, so assuming you're relaxed and your mind is receptive, see what enters your mind immediately after asking the question. Check in with them to see if you accurately picked up on anything.

Once you've built up from these exercises and think you are ready for a challenge, try mind reading next time you're on public transit or in a crowd somewhere. Do this as unobtrusively as you can. If you sense that someone's energy is really blocking you out and doesn't want to let anyone in, they want their privacy. Leave them be and try someone else who's perhaps more receptive. One common thing mind readers pick up on when reading minds are people's emotions. It's probably the easiest thing to access using telepathy, and you've probably read people's emotions telepathically before without even knowing it. It's important to distinguish body language and facial cues giving you information on someone, and telepathy providing that information. To remain unbiased and make sure telepathy is your only source of information, try to focus on someone's energy rather than looking at them/their appearance. You may focus on someone, trying to pick something up from them and feel a rush of worry wash over you. You may even pick up the reason why they are worried, though perhaps in a vague sense, and it may take more experience to get this specific.

In a way, mind reading is similar to psychometry, which we touched on in Chapter 2. You are trying to pick things up from a person: thoughts, emotions, images, etc. Except you can get a reading from them without actually touching them, which would be especially weird while practicing on a crowd of strangers in public.

What's important to remember with telepathy is that patience is key. It is not going to click overnight; in fact, it may take quite a while before you effectively get the hang of it, so don't be hard on yourself if you don't find that you are successful right away. You also may feel energetically drained after a session. Don't draw your practice out for too long as telepathy really works out your brain and it may exhaust you. If a message isn't going through, just plan to try it again another day. Don't deplete your mental power. And remember: when practicing either telepathic communication or mind reading, do not look at that person's face directly (if possible), as facial features and movements may cloud your judgment, mental focus, and force the reading or interpretation. Try to do it as best as possible using only your mind, so if you get it right, you can be sure it was telepathy, and there was no bias involved.

Chapter 6: Guided Meditation

As mentioned in the previous chapters, meditation is an invaluable tool for preparing yourself to use or flex your psychic abilities and to help when practicing and developing your gift. What it does is clear the mind and relax the body, putting you in a state of calm that makes it easier to focus on your spiritual abilities and the task you've set out for yourself. You can meditate even if you don't plan on using your power or practicing – it can also just be an everyday routine or habit that clears the mind of worries and improves your quality of life. Whatever the reason, let's take a look at some of the most effective methods of meditation and its uses in the next few paragraphs, and then we will get into the topic of guided meditation.

Meditation is a way to calm and clear your mind from distraction, clutter, and chatter. It has been used for thousands of years, but now more than ever it is important. As our attention spans are shorter and we are bombarded by information, activity, light, and color at every turn and from every angle, it is important for our brains to receive a moment of complete calm and relaxation, drowning out the noise and chaos in our lives.

To begin meditation, you, of course, need to set yourself up so that you're comfortable and calm. This means wearing comfortable, non-constricting clothes and finding a space that is quiet, peaceful and relaxing for you. You can play meditation music if you'd like, there are plenty of options online, and you can light incense if you feel like it would help. Decide how long you want to meditate for – usually, a shorter session of 15-20 minutes is recommended for beginners – and settle in. Focus on your breaths, in and out. Don't think about your breathing or try to analyze it; just let your focus lay with it, and nothing else. If any thoughts flit into your mind, acknowledge them but then let them drift away. Don't get stuck on any worries or plans; just see the thought, understand it, and then let it go – at least while you're meditating. The trick is to keep your mind clear and calm with no worldly distractions. It is inevitable that your mind will wander, especially as a beginner, but this is not a problem – just make sure to let each thought go and bring your focus right back around to your breathing. If it helps, you can have a chant or mantra playing in your head to help you focus on one thing and do away with worldly distractions. Repeating a word, mantra, or mental image of something calm will help you get into a trancelike state and get into that desired state of meditation. If you decide to focus on an image, pick something simple, something that makes you feel calm and unemotional. This could be a visualization technique as well. Make sure the position you are in will be comfortable for the length of your meditation as well – you don't want to get a cramp or have a limb fall asleep. This is a basic beginner's guide for meditation, in general, to give you some background. Now, we will get into a guided meditation, how to do it, and why it is beneficial.

Guided meditation specifically is one of the more recent branches of meditation. It's more or less self-explanatory. It's in the name – there is some form of a guide throughout your meditation. It can be a person in the room with you trained to guide you through your experience, or an audio or video recording or it can be written text. Whichever form you use, the purpose is to follow the instructions and questions during your meditation thoughtfully to reveal some insight to you and to elevate your energy. Often, there is peaceful and serene music played quietly in the background to help ease you into the meditation. Usually, the guide will use detailed imagery for most of it, and some of it you get to decide. If you've ever heard someone say, "I'm going to my happy place!" and close their eyes when in a stressful situation, they've likely created this happy place in their mind during a guided meditation. An example of something you might hear from a guided meditation is, "You are in a wide meadow. Look around. What color are the flowers? Is there a forest nearby?" These not only serve to create peaceful escapes and a refuge from life's stressful moments, but also your choices are sometimes analyzed at the end of the guided meditation to reveal something about who you are as a person, what decision you should make on something, or insight into your current emotional state. Another aspect that could be used in a guided meditation is focusing on the body. The guide may tell you to focus on different body parts and check whether or not they are relaxed, how they feel, and to relax them if they are not already. They may ask what sensations you feel in your body and in specific locations. This helps relax the physical self – a part of meditation that is also important. Guided meditations can be so relaxing that, occasionally, people may fall asleep during the experience. If you want to remain awake for the entire meditation, try leaning up against something comfortable rather than lying on your back, or if you're watching a video or listening to an audio meditation, try to watch the pictures that the video uses or pull up a nature slideshow online to watch along with. Just make sure it won't distract you from your meditative focus.

Your subconscious is at the forefront during these meditations. That is why the choices you make while in this deeply relaxed state can be analyzed and interpreted to reveal important information. The guide has created them for this purpose. The further along in the meditation, the further into this relaxed world you go, and the safer you feel. Your mind is open and vulnerable in this state – exactly how you need it to be for psychic work.

There are many free guided meditations on the internet; you don't have to see a specialist or leave the comfort of your home. They often have audio with a montage of eye-catching scenery and nature photos. You can watch the slideshow, or you can lie back and just listen. Many people choose to listen and follow guided meditations before they go to sleep, claiming it aids them in falling asleep easily and achieving a restful night's sleep.

You can also join a guided meditation class or do one-on-one sessions where you are guided through your meditation by a live instructor who is in the room with you. Depending on your personality, you may prefer one of these methods over the other, but if you are unsure, you can try both, live guide or online instruction, and see which way you prefer, or feels most comfortable and relaxing to you. After all, your relaxation is the whole point.

Not all guided meditations are created equal. There are many different forms, and they are useful for many different reasons. Some can be used to manifest different things like abundance and success. Some are used to improve and develop relationships, improving the self, and healing. The best ones to look up when it comes to aiding with psychic ability and development are the ones that work on inner peace and inner calm. Creating a quiet mind will improve your focus greatly.

In this age of technology, it's rare to find someone with a lengthier attention span who would jump at the chance to lie down and basically do nothing. Most of us would feel restless or bored. This isn't a bad thing necessarily; there is no right or wrong level of focus. However, this is a tool that's really worth struggling with that over. Try short meditations, at first, and work your way up. Do them before bed when you wouldn't have been doing anything anyways except staring at the wall until you fall asleep. This is a tool you're going to want to have in your collection, especially as an up and coming psychic with blossoming abilities that need to be sharpened and centered.

You will find that if you use guided meditations even somewhat regularly you will greatly improve your spiritual abilities and your mental and physical wellbeing will benefit on top of that. In today's fast-paced world, it's understandable if you don't always have the time, patience, or attention span to commit to sitting or lying down to a guided meditation. However, if you just make an effort and squeeze it in when you can, like before bed, it will do nothing but good. Once you make it into a habit, it will become easier to incorporate into your routine and pretty soon it will come as naturally as eating three meals a day and brushing your teeth in the morning. You will feel grateful and relieved at your newfound inner stillness, and your mind's usual chatter and babble will become more subdued (not eliminated – that isn't possible), reducing your overall stress level as well.

Chapter 7: Connecting with Spirit Guides

One aspect of meditation and spiritual work that we've touched on has been Spirit Guides and/or Guardian Angels. Spirit Guides are another invaluable tool for the psychic, whether you want to meditate to simply ground yourself and replenish your energy, draw more strength to yourself before you begin a reading, or whether you seek help/protection – these are all reasons to attempt to connect with your spirit guides and ask them for advice and strength. Always treat them with respect when making requests or asking something of them. Do not demand things from them, but do not be afraid or ashamed to ask for help, as we can't do everything alone. Treat them as you would a friend or mentor.

Spirit guides or guardian angels – whichever name you use the term is clear – are not deities that you must worship; they are a spiritual presence that watches over you and guides you. You do not need to fear some godly wrath – they are on your side and want the best for you!

There are a few different types of spirit guide. Your guide may take the form of an ancestor or loved one who has passed on from the physical realm but continues to watch over you. If they are an ancestor, they may be someone who died before you were born but there are certain signs that crop up that a relative who knew them will tell you means their presence is near – for example, if you had a grandmother who loved flowers, and flowers are a constant presence in your life, this may be a sign that this ancestor is watching over you. Ancestral Guides can go back many generations. You may not see the face of your ancient ancestor when connecting with them, but you will sense their relation and connection to you. You could also be watched over by a dear loved one who died during your life. This would most likely be someone who died earlier in your life as spirit guides tend to watch over you for your whole life, but it could be someone who passed on later as well.

Another common type of spirit guide are the ones that come in the form of animals. These are called 'animal guides'. You will likely be guided throughout your life by multiple different animal guides, each having something different to show or teach you – you won't just have one animal spirit that's assigned to you. Animal guides are often considered symbolic, or energies that embody the spirit of whichever animal it is that represents them. If you see a vision of a fierce panther while meditating, this Spirit Guide may offer protection and advice on assertiveness. If you see a bull calmly standing in a field, it may be there to help steady you.

Your spirit guide may not be ancestor nor show itself as any symbolic representation. It may just be pure energy, often seen as a brilliant light. This is what many people refer to as an angel. It is likely a comforting and familiar energetic entity that has watched over you since your conception. Make sure any entity you are connecting with truly is your spirit guide. If there is any feeling of darkness or discomfort, then that entity is not your spirit guide. Your only experience with your guide/s should be positive – that's how you know for sure.

Now that you know the basics of what a spirit guide is, let's look at how we can reach out and contact/communicate with our guides. This may be your first time interacting with your guide – you may not even know what form your guide will take yet!

Meditation is most people's go-to way to contact their spirit guide. There are many guided meditations (see Chapter 6) available online for contacting your spirit guide. If you're not doing a guided meditation, when you sit down to meditate, make your only focus contacting your spirit guide. If you are contacting them for a reason, you can also focus on the reason you wish to communicate with them, but at the beginning, just focus your purpose on meeting your spirit guide. Clear your mind and don't force anything. Like with every aspect of spirituality, don't be frustrated if it doesn't work right away. Just keep sitting down to meditate with the powerful intention of contacting your spirit guide. They may not appear to you in a vision or as an image, but if you keep your mind clear and let it flow naturally, you will begin to sense their presence, and over time your communication channel with them will become stronger.

You can contact your spirit guide through meditation, but sometimes they will show themselves to you without you being in a meditative state or reaching out to them, such as a crow swooping down to stand directly in the middle of the path you were walking down, eyes fixed on you, or your grandmother's scent suddenly filling your nostrils for a moment or hearing a song that you always associated with your uncle who passed away. These could all be the presence of your spirit guide.

Certain times, when your intuition strongly urges you to do or not do something, so clear it almost sounds like an inner voice is speaking to you (similar to clairaudience), this could be your Guardian Angel, giving advice or warnings in your day-to-day waking life. You don't have to do anything to experience this communication; just listen and acknowledge the advice. Your guide, in the spirit realm, likely knows things that you don't and has wisdom you may not, so it's always a good idea to trust them – but at the end of the day, it's your decision to make. They are guides, not dictators.

Your spirit guide/s may visit you and show themselves to you in the form of a dream. If you've ever had a particularly vivid dream where a benign entity (whether your dead grandmother, an animal, or an energetic presence) has spoken to you, signaled to you, or led you to something/somewhere, and you remember it clearly the next day, or at least you remember the essence of what they were communicating and showing to you, this was likely a visit from a spirit guide. Though you may remember the figures you encountered and what was communicated to you when you wake up, you are likely to forget important details – if not your whole dream as the day goes by –, so it's a good idea to keep a dream journal and write down exactly what you dreamed about in as much detail as you can remember after waking up. If you have to rush out the door to work, you can write in the notepad on your phone – it doesn't need to be anything fancy. If you want to keep a record of spirit guide encounters, symbolic, and important dreams, you can copy it into a paper journal when you get a chance. If you want to plan to meet a spirit guide during your dream, focus on a question you want answering or the reason you wish to contact them before you go to sleep. As you drift into sleep with this in mind as your focus, hopefully, you will encounter them in your dream that night. This is a system of lucid dreaming, so keep in mind that it may take a few tries to have this sort of control over your dreams.

No matter what form your spirit guide takes, and what purpose they're there for, it's possible to create a strong connection and channel of communication with them through practice. Remember: if an entity that you think is your spirit guide makes you feel negatively in any way or is surrounded by any dark or unpleasant energy, that is NOT your spirit guide, and you should disconnect from them. Your interactions with spirit guides should always be positive – if somewhat introspective, or if they're a dead loved one's spirit, then possibly bittersweet. Your spirit guide and/or guardian angel only wants the best for you, and they can be a great source of support that you shouldn't hesitate to draw on.

Chapter 8: Auras and Aura Reading

What exactly is an *aura*? You've surely heard the term before, but it may not be clear what it is exactly. Basically, every single person has one. In fact, all living beings do, but we're going to focus on us, humans. It's the energy field around people that gives you a feel for who they are as a person. Auras can be seen as colorful light emanating from somebody or energy sensed from somebody without touching them that can tell you information about the individual's personality. Reading auras can be tricky and requires practice to master it.

A person's aura can show up as a color or multiple colors surrounding a person's body. To practice seeing someone's aura, you could ask a friend if they could stand in front of a white background. It doesn't have to be their whole body, just head and shoulders are fine if you don't have a large enough background. This is the best way for a beginner to practice as the neutral background will make any colors that appear around them pop out clearly. Other colors can be distracting and cause bias, so ask them to wear the most neutral clothing possible. Try not to be in an environment you think will distract you or cause you to lose focus. Now that you've set this up, the way you will begin to see the colors of their aura is by choosing one spot to stare at (something on or near your friend that isn't colorful) and defocus your eyes slightly so that your vision is somewhat blurred. Don't concentrate on the spot you've chosen but instead on your peripheral view. Keep staring, it may take a few minutes, or it may show up right away, but you should begin to see a sort of light around your friend, sort of like an imprint or glowing form. Soon after, it should change from being just light to show a color. This is considered their aura. Make a note of what color (or colors) you saw, and you and your friend can look up what that color means, what it says about your friend and different interpretations of that color. Remember, color symbolism isn't universal, but see which one suits your friend the most, or you can interpret the color yourselves. In general, red can indicate an energetic individual, blue a good communicator, those with purple auras are mysterious, yellow could indicate a cerebral quality, green for creativity, orange is associated with generosity, and pink auras show a caring figure. Remember these are just basic, general and common interpretations. If you feel something else to be true, then so be it. Also, if you look away from your subject and see their imprint in front of you still, like how if you stare at the sun you'll see a glowing blue orb in your vision for a while, understand that this is NOT the person's aura. The aura is only the colors you saw surrounding your friend. If you spend time in a classroom or office with lots of blank colorless walls, you can practice on your classmates/coworkers in your day-to-day life. Just don't let them catch you staring! It may be hard to explain.

As well as seeing someone's aura, it is also possible to sense someone's aura energetically. This is slightly easier than seeing the aura, and you've likely sensed someone's aura in the past unwittingly. You can first practice sensing auras with yourself, and your own energetic presence. It's easy, and there are two ways of doing this. The first way is to rub your palms together to stimulate them, and then hold them apart from each other (palms facing each other). Slowly begin bringing them closer together, noticing the energy you feel, the changes, the increase in energy as you bring them closer together. The other way is similar. Press your palms together with some strength for 30 seconds to a minute. Then pull them apart, and slowly bring

them back into each other, the same as in the first method. In both methods, notice how you could sense the energy of your palms the closer they got, even though they weren't touching at all?

Next, you can try reading the aura of someone else. Ask a friend to stand or sit in front of you. You can either ask them to close their eyes while you run your hands close to their body but never touching, or close your eyes and have them do this to you. Either way, you are merging auras. As a beginner, you should start with your hands closer to the body, but as you develop your skills, try from farther away. If your friend is moving their hands into your aura, it's the same principle. Get them to start close so you can really sense it, and then try from farther away. What you're most likely to feel is tingling, but you may pick up on the person's feelings and emotional state. While doing this, see if your mood changes and what sensations you pick up. Have you noticed an increase or decrease in energy? A sudden mood change or strong emotion? This is likely seeping from the other person's aura into yours as they are combined. If you felt only a tingling or nothing at all, that's fine. You're a beginner, so don't expect full results on the first try. If you felt any other sensations or feelings discuss them with your friend. Ask them if this is what they were/are feeling and thus if you are correct in surmising their mental state. If you'd like, keep a record of your experiences and practice sessions of aura reading in your journal.

Aura reading both visually and energetically is a useful skill for the psychic because it helps you get a sense of the person you're doing a reading for – what they're like as a person and what their current emotional and mental state is. You can pick up on any worries or reservations they may have, as well as what mood they're in coming into the reading. Having this knowledge can help you tailor the reading to the subject. As a psychic, you'll find that no two people, and therefore no two readings, will be the same. You may want to use different techniques, tools, and ways of explaining premonitions to someone based on the insights you have picked up from them.

Your aura is your energy field. It is a reflection of yourself and your current state of being. It can be weighed down and get clogged with negative energies, so here's how to cleanse and refresh it.

First, you'll want to imagine your aura. You don't need to necessarily see any particular colors or light in your mind's eye, but just visualize it around you and focus on this knowledge that an energy field surrounds you. You should be relaxed, and your eyes should be closed while doing this. Now, think of what negative interactions or thoughts you may have had or may have been directed towards you recently. Hanging on to these interactions is usually one of the big causes of aura blockage. Let them go. If you have to bring it up to someone and apologize or have an honest conversation with them, then do so. If not, then there is no reason for you to be carrying it with you. Imagine on every exhale you are letting go of a negative thought, worry, or stressor from your mind. Every time you inhale, you are reenergizing and reinvigorating your aura, bringing a renewed feeling to your once cluttered energy field, which is now a blank space again. You obviously can't eliminate everything from your aura; otherwise, there would be no essence of yourself in it anymore. What you're trying to do with this exercise is release all the negative clutter that can build up over time and make you feel dragged down, low in energy and even depressed. Do this exercise a few times to really clear out all the stagnation. You can find your own visualization technique – whatever will work best and be most effective for you. And try and take breaks from the chaos of life and responsibility. Spend extra time in nature or someplace that will make you feel comfortable and at peace.

Your aura may also be stagnant because you are in a stagnant spot in your life. Do some deep digging and introspection to see if you can get to the bottom of this. Is there some aspect of your life that you don't like? Do you feel unfulfilled? Is it time for a change? No amount of deep breathing is going to answer these questions. If you think they are applicable to how you feel, you're going to have to tackle them, no matter how hard it may be. For your own wellbeing, you need to get to the bottom of what aspect of your life needs an adjustment. If you remain stuck energetically like this, it will also hinder your psychic abilities, making you feel too lethargic or low in energy to practice with your gift effectively. Take care of your aura as you would take care of your physical self. Treat your aura's blockages as you would treat an illness or a broken bone.

Chapter 9: Mediumship

So far, we've talked about psychic reading. In this chapter, we will talk about medium reading. So what's the difference? Well, someone who does psychic readings may not have mediumistic abilities, which are acting as a vessel and a bridge of communication between the spirit world and the world of the living – but all mediums have psychic abilities, as this is what they use to contact the spirits of the dead.

Mediumship or mediums may be a term you haven't heard before. As mentioned above, a medium is a person who is a bridge between the dead and the living. They can communicate with those that have passed over and convey messages to the living for them. If you've ever used a Ouija board, this is one form of mediumship, as you are contacting, or attempting to contact, the spirits of the dead – although Ouija boards are usually used as a form of entertainment more than anything serious.

The forms of mediumship used by practicing mediums are when the spirit of the dead speaks through the medium, and when the medium receives messages clairvoyantly (or clairsentiently, claircognizantly, clairaudiently) and relays the message to the living. Most often the medium is asked by a living person to try and contact and create a channel of communication with a dead loved one because they miss them and/or because there is unfinished business or unanswered questions between them and they want a sense of closure. The spirit of the dead loved one likely feels the same so that these sessions can be very healing.

If you wish to become a medium, an intermediary between the spirit world and the living, you will need to have a strong hold on the four intuitive types (even if you favor one more than the others) as the messages will come through, and you will perceive them via clairvoyance, clairaudience, clairsentience or claircognizance. This is something to try once you've been practicing your psychic abilities for a while and feel confident. You can still be on a beginner's path, but make sure you've got the basics down. If you feel that you are a natural psychic medium, someone who has sensed the presence of spirits of the dead from a young age, then you may already have an idea of how to communicate and use these spirit channels. This is not a necessity to becoming a medium, however.

If you know any mediums, or if you find that there is a local practicing medium you can get in touch with, ask them about their craft. How does it feel to communicate with spirits? When did they start or when did they first notice they had this ability? What are some examples of mediumistic experiences they've had? You can also search online to read first-hand experiences from mediums if there are none you can contact where you live. Just be careful that the person you are learning from is not a scam artist, as the world of psychic practice is rife with frauds looking to exploit people for money.

To begin practice towards contacting spirits, you must be in a state of total relaxation. Find a calm, comfortable spot, without bright lights. Feel the energy of the universe flowing through you, and relax your mind, letting other thoughts that poke at you to fade away. Now it's time to call upon the spirits. Before you do this next step, make sure you've mastered psychic protection against negative spirits and entities as it's possible to accidentally invite a negative spirit into your home (see Chapter 3 for more information). To help reduce the risk of a negative spirit entering your space, think of a specific deceased loved one of yours that you would like to contact (this can also be a pet). That way your call is not extended to any spirit who happens to be around. They are not invited, only your loved one's spirit is. Now call upon them out loud. Ask them into your space and maybe ask a question of them or ask if they have anything to communicate. Call upon them mentally too. Summon up an image of them in your mind, quite detailed, and mentally welcome them into space. If you feel their presence, ask them a question you have prepared beforehand. You may sense them in different ways, whether you smell the cologne they used to wear, hear their laugh or a song they used to sing, see their favorite color or a piece of clothing they used to wear in your mind's eye, or a sudden shift of emotion where you feel warm and full of love. These are just examples to show you that the way you sense them may not be seeing their image speaking to you in your mind's eye. The way they answer the questions may be through images that must be interpreted or through words you see or hear in your mind. If you answer a question and get a strong emotion immediately afterward, this may also be a response. Or if they answer claircognizantly, then you will just know the answer. Remember not to force or make up their presence or answers. Just let them flow, and if they don't show up or answer any questions, then that's okay. Just keep reaching out and practicing and stay relaxed. If you pick up nothing, don't force it. Release and try again another time.

You can also try practicing as a medium for a friend, and you can call upon the spirit of their loved one, asking the spirit any questions your friend may have of them. If you really want to challenge yourself, don't ask your friend who the person they want to contact us. Go in blind. Ask them only to picture and think about the person they wish to contact. Keep your mind clear and relaxed, and be open and receptive to any energies and messages you may receive. If images or feelings start popping up, describe them to your friend. You can go online and look up videos of psychics in action to see how this is done. For example, if you're sitting there with an empty mind and all of a sudden, a figure of a man pops into your mind, and then the color red, and then the concept of Thanksgiving dinner, and the smell of cigarettes you would say, "I'm seeing a man, now the color red, and something to do with Thanksgiving. I also smell cigarettes." You obviously will not know what this means, so ask your friend if it has any significance for them. After all, when acting as a medium, the message isn't for you but for the other person, the one the spirit of the dead is connected to. If this is a legitimate message your friend will get it right away, and if they feel like it, they can tell you what it means to them. Maybe the man was their uncle whose favorite color or shirt or car was red, and he always hosted a big family Thanksgiving at his house – it was an annual family tradition. And he smoked which was a familiar and comforting reminder of his presence to all who knew him. This is an example of how a medium reading may progress. You may hear words or phrases from the deceased as well which you should relay to the living person. Tell them everything you see and hear in your message, even if it may not make sense to you, as it may make sense and be important to them. If not, then just keep going. You probably won't get everything right, especially since you are just beginning, so just keep telling them what you are sensing and make sure you aren't forcing these messages. Make sure they are coming to you naturally and clearly from the spirit you have contacted.

Chapter 10: Dream Interpretation

So far, we've talked about the conscious efforts you can make to invite psychic prediction, but half the time, it's your unconscious mind that's at the helm. Dreams can be a way for the universe, your spirit guides, or even your own subconscious to reveal important messages to you. Anyone can receive meaningful dreams, but you'll notice the more you become in tune with your psychic abilities and the universe, the more you will receive these messages. The interpretation of dreams has been practiced for centuries in all manner of ancient societies, and it is still used frequently today.

So how do you tell if your dream is trying to tell you something or if it's important at all? Well, usually, some element or elements stand out clearly and vividly and make an impression on you while you're in the dream, and that you remember when you wake up. If you forget the dream, the chances are it wasn't important. Sometimes there will be a figure that will directly tell you something that you will remember when you wake up. Often, however, it is not so clear.

There may be a series of events that happen or an overall feeling throughout the dream that may be associated with some aspect of the dream, or maybe there are people or animals or anything symbolic that you see or interact with. These can all be interpreted and ascribed to your waking life. Remember that if anything in your dream really stands out to you, there's probably something to learn from it.

If there is a figure in your dream telling you something, how they appear to you may be just as symbolic and important as the message they delivered. If in your dream you are led by a deer from the darkness of the woods into a bright and sunny clearing, the message here is easily interpreted to mean you are very stressed and in need of peace of mind (or you are about to enter a metaphorical "eye of the storm" in your life). But the deer has significance too. If you were led by the person you were in love with or a bird or your childhood pet, these could all put a different spin on the dream's meaning and how you interpret it. If your partner led you, this might signify that if you keep moving through this rough patch, you will be rewarded – you are on a path to this haven together. A bird may signify anxiety or restlessness, a need for freedom. A childhood pet leading you may make the clearing mean your past/your childhood that you have a deep nostalgia and longing for at this time in your life. The steadiness and silence of the deer, as well as its innocent (non-predator) nature and instinctive knowledge of the forest, may be telling you to keep your head up and keep calm and you'll get there. Of course, there are many ways to interpret these things and it also depends on the other context in the dream as well as your life. However, as you've probably noticed, there are many similarities between interpreting dreams and interpreting premonitions.

An important thing to remember when interpreting your dream is to try to do it without bias. This will create the most accurate interpretation, and the most honest. It's also best not to use outside sources like dream dictionaries or dream a-z websites or books unless you're really stuck. If you do feel like you're not getting the full picture, you can describe your dream to someone you know. Even if they have no psychic interest or have never interpreted a dream before, they may see the picture clearly. Say, for example, you dreamt of a bear fishing by the river with her cubs. The cubs fall into the river and are swept away, but the mother doesn't try to save them. Then the dream switches to the cubs back safe and sound with the mother bear. You just can't figure it out, so you ask your friend, and they ask if you've felt distanced or disconnected from your mother recently? Or (if you're a mother) if you've felt that you haven't been taking care of your children and feel inadequate? Right away this clicks for you, and you wonder why you didn't see it before. Always go to a friend or family member for help interpreting if you're stuck BEFORE turning to a dream dictionary, as dream dictionaries don't know all the details of your dream, often providing vague interpretation of one-word symbols, and they don't know the context of your life.

The technique of journaling has been discussed many times throughout this book, but again, it's a good practice to keep a journal of your dreams. Writing down a dream as soon as you wake up helps you remember and lock in details that would otherwise be forgotten soon after waking, and even if you do forget, you can go back and reread it and, hopefully, it will evoke the memory of the dream again. As well as helping to remember, it will also allow you to keep track of any patterns that crop up in your dreams and analyze them. If you think a dream is important, always write it down in as much detail as you can remember – everything counts. You can even add a little sketch if you can't put something into words fully.

Another way to start analyzing your dream is by questioning it. Why did I see that person in that context? Why were buffalo present throughout my dream? Why was there a feeling of uneasiness and discordance even though my dream was peaceful? What was the setting of my dream? What was I trying to do? Who was I in the dream? Why was the bright red bird that appeared briefly so vivid?

These are a few examples, but feel free to ask any questions you think are relevant to your dream.

One common theme in dreams that people fear is death. Whether it be their own or the death of a loved one, but don't worry – dreaming of death isn't predicting it. Dreams are rarely premonitions and are more commonly reflections of your emotional state and metaphors for what is going on in your life and what you need to deal with. If you dream of death, this may signify massive change or emotional/spiritual rebirth on your horizon. Maybe you're moving, or taking a trip, finishing school, experiencing a breakup, etc. It may also mean a part of you has symbolically died and that inner transformation is in the works. Death is often a symbol of change in our lives. In fact, in tarot, readers often tell the client whom they are reading for not to take the death card literally. Take a look at who or what is dying in your dream and ask yourself why. Why is this person dying, and what do they represent or symbolize as a part of my life? How does this death fit into the context of my life? Even if the person who dies is someone you know, this can still be a representation of a part of yourself or your relationship with them. It could also more literally indicate a fear of losing this person. There are many ways of interpreting death dreams, and almost none of them mean that someone is literally going to die, so put your mind at ease and do some introspection or prepare for some big changes ahead.

Another common dream theme is being chased, stalked or attacked. Often, the dreamer will feel as if they are trying to move but can't or can only move in slow motion. It can be any villain, creature or animal chasing or attacking you, or you may not know what is chasing you, but you can sense yourself being pursued throughout your dream. Often dreams like this are closer to nightmares and can cause extreme fear and anxiety for the sleeping person, especially if you know your assailant plans to harm or kill you (or they are already doing so if the dream involves you being attacked). This may represent anxiety or fear you have in your day-to-day life. It can be very literal, such as being attacked by a dog and you are scared of dogs or being chased by someone who has caused you harm in the past. However, it can also be symbolic, such as being chased by your boss whom you are intimidated by in real life and fear will fire you soon. Or being chased/attacked by an animal whose traits represent things you fear – for example, being chased by an owl may not seem like a very frightful situation, but owls are silent, solitary and adept hunters so this could represent communication issues or relationship issues or a fear of being alone. Try to hold it up to the context of your life, and really question and dig deep into why that specific entity was pursuing and/or attacking with the intention of harming you. Attacking dreams specifically can show vulnerability and a feeling of loss of control in your life. Pursuit and attack dreams may not represent outside forces at all and could be showing you that you need to take some time for introspection – your feelings could be what is really "attacking" or "chasing" you, and inner turmoil may be at the root of these disturbing dreams.

Being naked or just in your underpants/inappropriate clothes is another classic theme to dream about. The most obvious interpretation we can get from this is a feeling of vulnerability, feeling too exposed and metaphorically naked. It can also be linked to a feeling of loss of control and anxiety, or it could point to a need to be liked and a fear that not everyone likes you, that you are judged by others (whether this is true or not). Something else to consider is: if you are hiding anything or have any secrets, this dream may reflect that you feel everyone knows. The bottom line is these dreams are known to indicate insecurity of some sort, so take a look at what is happening in your dream or who is in the dream and seeing you naked or not seeing you. This is likely a reflection of who or what makes you insecure in your waking life. If it isn't obvious just take a look straight away at your life and think of areas where you are insecure. Maybe you quite literally are insecure about your body and enjoy the safety of hiding it beneath layers of clothes. There may be areas that you haven't even thought about. These are spots where you need to work on and build up your confidence – a message which a dream of this sort was trying to convey to you. On the other hand, if you felt good and positive about being naked or semi-naked, then this is a good sign! You are likely feeling very confident and empowered in your life at the current moment and feel free as though nothing can stop you. Again, one literal meaning of this dream could be that you are very comfortable and confident with your body and are not insecure about its appearance. It can indicate that you are happy with yourself as a person and don't feel the need to seek validation from others.

Falling is another common dream. This is another dream that can indicate a feeling of loss of control and be overwhelmed in your life, especially if you feel negative and if there's a feeling of fear and anxiety as you're falling. It could be a fear of failure in anything from work, school, relationships – or it could be just a fear of the inability to keep up with your life. It may also symbolize a feeling of disillusionment with something, some aspect of your life or someone in your life. Ask yourself how you felt when you were falling. Was anyone else around before/during/after your fall? Where did you fall from? And what else was happening in the dream? Try and answer these questions and interpret their meaning in relation to your life.

You've probably heard already that teeth falling out is one of the most common, if not THE most common dream. Almost everyone has at one time dreamt of their teeth falling out. Since this is such a common dream, there are many different interpretations. One possible interpretation is that a major life change is coming. For a kid or teenager to dream about their teeth falling out is a sign of their coming maturity and path to adulthood. The loss of teeth is associated with the loss of something/some part of your life. With the example of the children, it would represent the loss of childhood. Dreams of teeth falling out can also represent insecurity, inability to make decisions, or dissatisfaction with some aspect of your life that you feel unable to change. If your teeth fall out quite rapidly, it's possible that you are feeling overwhelmed by something in your life or just can't find a solution to something. On the positive side, teeth falling out can mean success and prosperity is yours or is coming into your life. It can also indicate a positive life change or a change you are ready to face head-on, or that will come about with ease. The key to deciphering whether or not a dream of your teeth falling out should be interpreted positively or negatively is by examining how you felt during the dream. You likely won't feel necessarily *good* about your teeth falling out, but if you felt neutral or calm, this can be interpreted in a positive way – a positive change for the better or success on your horizon. If you felt scared and anxious about your teeth falling out, this may represent something more negative and be a cause for some introspection as well as looking at what aspects of your day-to-day life could cause these feelings. Maybe it's time to make a tough decision or come to terms with an unwanted life change.

Flying is a common dream that many people are thrilled to dream about. Who hasn't wished they could fly at some point in their life? The dream world is the only space where we can fly uninhibited, with no machinery to aid us. So, what does it mean? Well, for starters, dreams of flying are usually positive, accompanied by feelings of happiness and euphoria. This can be your mind's way of easing some of the worries that weigh down your mind, as sleep is your only escape from them (though we now know that they can follow you into your dreams in disturbing ways). A positive dream about flying shows that you are focused on achieving goals you have in your life – whether you are close to achieving them or not, the fact is that you are confident in yourself and believe that you can accomplish them. A dream of flying can also indicate emotional stability, and peace of mind. It may be a reflection of getting out of something or completing a task that was metaphorically weighing you down, and now you are free. It can also represent empowered decision making. It can also indicate that you may need to look at things from a different perspective or need to see the bigger picture. If you feel negative about flying or get nervous and want to land and be on stable ground again, this could mean you are reluctant to allow any big changes in your life, preferring to stick to the comforts, routine, and habits of your comfort zone. Something may feel out of alignment in your life, and you don't like it, preferring everything to go back to normal. Though it's hard to control your dreams, try and ease up a little and relax within your dream next time you dream you are scared of flying. Enjoy the thrill and the rush instead of feeling nervous, exposed and out of place. This may help manifest those feelings in your waking life, in whatever area you may need to relax and accept some change into.

Being late to something is a dream everyone has at least once. Usually, this one is quite literal. The dreaming person is anticipating some big event in their life, work, school, a date, etc., that they cannot be late for or miss, and likely have to wake up early and set an alarm for. Dreaming of being late, sleeping in, your alarm not going off, or missing something entirely is usually because you have been worrying about making sure you get to this event on time. Often, the dream will be centered around the event itself, and you will wake up relieved that you haven't missed it. Symbolically, a dream like this can be telling you that there's too much on your plate and that you can't possibly keep up with it all. It's telling you to maybe take it easy with the commitments in your life and maybe take on less. Dreaming of being late can reflect a feeling of being overwhelmed in your life, usually juggling too much at once and thus creating a sense of chaos. Try to see what commitments and activities you can cut down on and where you can add some extra "me time" to your daily routine. You may feel a lot of pressure and demand from work, school, or your home life. Sometimes it's hard to create time for yourself in today's fast-paced society, but it's best to listen to your subconscious. If there's something that can be moved or cut out to create that space, do it. A need for change is clear. Just because you can multitask doesn't mean you should! These dreams may also indicate a problem with authority if, in the dream, you do not care or feel anxious about being late for some work or school appointment (or anything with an authority figure in your life) or you are late on purpose.

Dreaming of driving or being in an out of control car is also a classic dream. This dream has a fairly obvious interpretation. Some aspect of your life is out of control. Something in your life is snowballing faster and faster and you either have *no* control over what's happening, or you *feel* that you have no control over what's happening. The car and the road are usually representing you and your path in life. So something in your life path is taking over, and you have no way of stopping it. If you are not in the driver's seat and there is no one else in the car, then this means it is your responsibility that things got so out of hand and your responsibility to get things back on track. If someone else is behind the wheel, then be careful if this person is also a part of your waking life. The dream could be warning you that this person is a bad influence or is leading your path astray. It could be trying to tell you that this person is manipulating you and they don't have your best interests at heart. They may even mean to cause you harm. Do not let this person control your metaphorical car, and keep an eye on them in your waking life. Notice your interactions and the actions of the other person towards you. However, dreams of out of control cars aren't always bad. If you are a child starting to mature and enter the next phase of your life, then dreaming that you suddenly have to enter the driver's seat and attempt to take control over this out of control car (this is a common dream for children because kids have never driven), this can be symbolic of you entering the unknown world of adulthood, unsure of many norms, and how to proceed. This is especially telling if, at one moment, the child's parents were in the front seat and then they suddenly disappear and it's up to the child to steer the car. This is reflected in their reality because now it is up to them to do many of the things they relied on their parents to do. They have more responsibilities. When dreaming of an out of control car, ask yourself how you feel. Who is or isn't in the car with you? Are you alone? What's the setting? And what was happening before/after the car lost control? These are what to look at and hold up in comparison to your own life.

A natural disaster is perhaps a slightly less common dream, but the message is usually very important. Dreaming of a natural disaster does not mean that disaster is going to strike in your waking life, so don't worry – don't take it too literally. The most common meaning for a natural disaster (earthquake, storm, lightning, hurricane, tornado, volcano, tsunami, etc.) dream is emotional repression. It can be a very general symbol of emotional repression, or it could get more specific. For example, a dream of a volcano or lightning bolt could represent pent-up anger, while a flood or monsoon could be unacknowledged repressed sadness or even depression. A violent, chaotic storm could symbolize anger again, or restless aggression and/or energy that has no outlet in your day-to-day life. Earthquakes can be telling you the same, and they could also mean frustration. Another thing dreaming of a natural disaster could signify is a massive life change or upheaval of some sort – usually, a positive change in most cases.

Keep an eye out for the four elements (water, earth, fire, and air) showing up in your dreams. Think about how the element shows up in your dream, what it is known to represent, and how you feel in your dream in relation to seeing it.

Water dreams are usually to do with emotion. A dream of water is likely telling you something about your emotional state in your present reality. How does the water appear to you? How do you interact with it, and what are your feelings towards it? Calm and crystal-clear waters signify emotional clarity, peace of mind, and stability. If the water is murky or muddy, however, this means there is an aspect of your life, most likely rooted in emotion, that is indecipherable to you at the moment – something you may have been grappling with for a while and just can't figure out. Dark and deep water shows very deep emotion. Perhaps you have recently fallen in love or lost a loved one or experienced some sort of major emotional event in your life. These could be emotions on a subconscious level as well that you are not aware of. If you fear water in your dream, you are likely having a hard time coming to terms with how you feel about something and your emotions in your waking life. Dreaming about a terrifying ocean storm or tsunami can indicate your metaphorical dam is about to burst. Emotions that have been repressed are bubbling up. It can also mean you feel very out of control about a part of your life – like you have no grasp on events that occur. Seeing a tsunami in a dream means you should brace yourself for things to come in your waking life. Dreams of drowning can also be a sign of a fear to face and deal with emotions. Water dreams can also show that we have a need to cleanse ourselves, and our spirit. It wouldn't symbolize that your subconscious literally wants you to clean yourself or take a shower physically, but it may be suggesting that more of an emotional and spiritual cleansing/healing is in order, especially if you've dealt with any kind of emotional trauma or crisis recently. Or even in the past and those feelings have just been building up. Water can also be a major symbol of rebirth and taking on a new challenge or chapter in your life. Entirely new beginnings and new possibilities may be coming up for you.

A few of the words associated with fire are anger, passion, love, aggression, heat, destruction, and energy. A dream about fire can indicate many things depending on the context – like the type of fire, how you felt, what the fire was doing, and how you were involved. Fire dreams can often have something to do with rebirth, just as water does. Just look at what fire does in nature. Yes, it can be destructive, but it burns away the old to make way for new growth. A dream with fire could symbolize letting things go and letting yourself and your spirit grow and mature. The symbol of the phoenix rising from the ashes is a perfect metaphor for the positive sign the element of fire can mean for you in a dream. If something in your dream is being consumed by fire and you feel upset about it, however, this can mean that you are being consumed by your (likely more negative) emotions in your waking life. Examine yourself for unchecked rage, obsession, jealousy, restlessness, etc. Try and find a healthy outlet for these emotions in your life so that they don't get built up and have a negative influence on your mental, spiritual and emotional state. The more controlled the fire in your dream is, the more stable your emotions and life are. The more out of control fire, the more it may be a sign of big change, or a hint to rein in some of your emotional outbursts and passions somewhat. If you are not someone who is passionate and outwardly expresses your emotions, then an out of control fire can be interpreted as your subconscious coming to the breaking point with repressed emotions, and you *do* need to let it out somehow, but be cautious. Just letting loose could have negative effects on your life. Think things through and don't do or say anything you'll regret later. Maybe try some introspection and talking to someone trusted and removed from your situation or feelings, even a professional if you think it requires this level of advice. Fire is a sign of impulse, so be careful not to be too impulsive. This goes double if you are already an impulsive person. However, remember, unless you feel negative about the fire in your dream, you don't need to fear it despite its negative reputation. Think of a phoenix rising from the ashes again. More often than not, fire is a positive symbol in dreams.

Dreaming about the earth element, so anything involving dirt, the ground, trees, mountains, and nature, in general, can be interpreted in many ways, as it takes many forms. It can also be less noticeable to us when dreaming, despite its frequent occurrence in our dreams, because it is always there in the form of the ground we stand on. This isn't the only form it takes, however, as it is a very versatile element – so let's take a look at some of its more symbolic appearances in dreams. Earth is different from the other three elements as it is the only solid. Grounding, stability, and the material or physical realm are what it represents in general. It is also a symbol of stubbornness, rigidness, and an unchanging spirit. The one time that earth can represent rebirth in dreams is if you dream or see in your dream something just starting to grow or blossom out of the earth, or any kind of new growth. Earth being the symbol of materialism, this could mean the growth of success and prosperity, usually financial. However, the earth is also the symbol for mother earth/mother nature, so this could symbolize fertility or richness of life. Being stuck in the mud or being sucked down and swallowed by the earth could symbolize financial difficulty or a feeling of being overwhelmed with everything that you have to do in your life at the moment, especially if a feeling of fear accompanies this. Being within the earth in some way, entering a cave, underground space or tunnel, could indicate that you are exploring and becoming more aware of your subconscious. You are becoming aware or made aware of something hidden from your conscious mind. This is usually a good sign and can be a signifier of personal growth. Sometimes these dreams can be frightening though. If you feel scared when going underground in a dream, this may be attributed to the fact that there is something there that you don't want to face. There is something you buried in your subconscious that you don't want to see or deal with. That is usually what these dreams mean.

Air, like earth, is less noticeable in dreams than fire and water are. This is because earth and air are bound to be in our dreams time and time again – like the air we breathe and the ground we stand on. However, it can take on other forms as well as this less noticeable appearance. Hence, let's take a look at how else it appears in our dreams and what it can mean. Air represents intelligence, communication, and spirituality (although it can be said that every element has spiritual ties in one way or another, as they are all equally a part of our world). Harsh and gusting winds that leave you feeling unsettled and uncomfortable, or more negative emotions in a dream, can symbolize vulnerability. Perhaps you are feeling spiritually/emotionally vulnerable in your life, or perhaps you are not even aware of these vulnerabilities. We mentioned flying dreams and what they symbolize, but we'll touch on it here briefly as it falls under the air element. A dream of flying is more often than not positive, and if it is a positive flying dream, it represents peace of mind and a feeling of freedom. Maybe you've just paid off a debt or completed a task or ended/entered into a relationship. Maybe it is a more spiritual reason, but whatever is it, something in your life has likely caused you great peace of mind if you have a positive flying dream. Consider yourself lucky as flying dreams are some of the best dreams people can have. Air, like water and fire, is a very changeable flexible element. A great storm or wind can indicate a major life change as well as vulnerability. If there is a lack of air or it feels hard to breathe, you may feel panicked, anxious, and overwhelmed in your waking life. If the air is cold, this could indicate emotional distance/coldness, and/or loneliness or an unwanted distance from others you care about. Gusts of wind appearing negatively in your dream could also indicate that you have a need to ground yourself and get in touch with reality.

Remember, it's all symbolic – these dreams of the elements aren't premonitions about you drowning or being burned in a fire or getting swallowed by the earth or that a tornado is going to suck you away. If they come with negative feelings, then there is something in your life that is causing these significant and powerful dream messages – and interpreting them is a step in the right direction to figuring out how to get to the bottom of these feelings or issues, tackle them, grow, and move on.

Conclusion

Thank you for making it through to the end of *Psychic: The Ultimate Psychic Development Guide to Develop Abilities Such as Intuition, Clairvoyance, Telepathy, Healing, Aura Reading, Mediumship, and Connecting to Your Spirit Guides*! It should have been informative and provided you with all of the tools you need to achieve your goals – whatever they may be.

The next step is to go forth and start utilizing the tips, tricks, tools, and techniques provided in this book to begin realizing your psychic potential and to become confident and empowered as your journey into the world of psychic power progresses. As you become more confident in your abilities and begin to see more results, you will have the desire to attempt some of the more difficult techniques and psychic reading styles suggested and described in this book, such as telepathy, crystal ball scrying, mediumship, and aura reading. And remember: it's true what they say – practice really does make perfect! Hence, if something doesn't work for you right away, it doesn't mean that it won't work or that you cannot use that technique! Everyone can use any of the tools mentioned in this book – though, for some, it comes easier than for others. If you see someone who has started a beginner like you but are now better at using a certain practice, it may just come more naturally to them. Don't judge yourself and your progress based on others – just stick with it, and you'll see how far you progress. Moreover, there are likely to be things that come more naturally to you than to others, so don't worry – it evens out!

Finally, if you found this book useful in any way, a review on Amazon is always appreciated!

Check out more books by Kimberly Moon

And another one...

Made in the USA
Las Vegas, NV
10 September 2021